The combating terrorism community will be facing new challenges – expanding mission sets and reduced resources.

Terror networks are enlarging their labyrinths by embracing transnational criminal organizations, engaging in lawfare and economic warfare, and using social and traditional media to amplify their messages. At the same time, resources that were previously available to counter these irregular adversaries are being reduced or reallocated to address other national security threats.

The Combating Terrorism Technical Support Office (CTTSO) and its programs have existed for almost 30 years rapidly developing the capabilities needed by the combating terrorism community to execute its missions.

Elements charged with combating terrorism will need to increase their efforts to coordinate tactics, techniques, procedures, and technologies to reduce the impact of decreased resources. Increased use of working groups, exercises, and other collaborations are approaches that could assist. CTTSO interagency membership has expanded significantly since 2001. While the number of active projects has remained level, the end user participation on each project has dramatically increased leading to a wider dissemination of successful capabilities.

At the same time, CTTSO has expanded its avenues for the rapid development of capabilities. Prior innovative approaches to solving the requirements of operators in the field are becoming commonplace at CTTSO. By using commercial crowdsourcing pathways, prizes, and challenges, Small Business Innovation Research, the Rapid Innovation Fund, partners like In-Q-Tel, and traditional Broad Agency Announcements, CTTSO customers can gain access to possible game-changing and more cost effective solutions that were previously unavailable to government programs.

CTTSO strives to ensure the delivery of improved capabilities to our armed forces, law enforcement, and other first responders in an efficient manner, now and in the future.

DoD photo by Tech. Sgt. Michael R. Holzworth, U.S. Air Force/Released

Table of Contents

COMBATING TERRORISM TECHNICAL SUPPORT OFFICE

Mission

The mission of the CTTSO is to identify and develop capabilities to combat terrorism and irregular adversaries and to deliver these capabilities to Department of Defense components and interagency partners through rapid research and development, advanced studies and technical innovation, and provision of support to U.S. military operations.

```
┌─────────────────────────────────────────────────┐
│        Assistant Secretary of Defense for        │
│   Special Operations & Low-Intensity Conflict    │
└─────────────────────────────────────────────────┘
                        │
┌──────────────────┐    │    ┌──────────────────────┐
│ Department of State │       │   Combating Terrorism   │
└──────────────────┘         │ Technical Support Office │
                             └──────────────────────┘
                                        │
┌──────────────────┐  ┌──────────────────────────┐  ┌──────────────────┐
│ Technical Support │  │ Explosive Ordnance Disposal │  │ Irregular Warfare │
│  Working Group    │  │   Low-Intensity Conflict    │  │     Support       │
└──────────────────┘  └──────────────────────────┘  └──────────────────┘
```

Organization

The Assistant Secretary of Defense for Special Operations/Low-Intensity Conflict (ASD (SO/LIC)) established CTTSO in 1999 to consolidate its research and development programs previously administered by the Office of the Assistant Secretary of Defense (Command, Control, Communications, and Intelligence). The research and development effort that supports the interagency Technical Support Working Group (TSWG) was the first program to transition to CTTSO. TSWG is divided into 10 subgroups, each chaired by senior representatives from federal agencies with special expertise in those functional areas. The Explosive Ordnance Disposal/Low-Intensity Conflict (EOD/LIC) Program, which develops advanced technologies for Joint Service EOD and Special Operations Forces (SOF) missions, transitioned in 2001. In 2007, the Irregular Warfare Support (IWS) Program was initiated to satisfy a growing need to improve the capacity of the United States to counter insurgencies and fight an irregular war.

The CTTSO and Other Agencies

The CTTSO is charged with providing a forum for interagency and international users to discuss mission requirements to combat terrorism, prioritize these requirements, fund and manage solutions, and deliver capabilities. The CTTSO accomplishes these objectives through rapid prototyping of novel solutions developed and field tested before the traditional acquisition systems are fully engaged. This low-risk approach encourages interdepartmental and interagency collaboration, thereby reducing duplication, eliminating capability gaps, and stretching development dollars.

The CTTSO accomplishes its mission in three ways. First, CTTSO takes operational requirements from warfighters, incorporates policy priorities of the Department of Defense (DoD) civilian leadership[1], and rapidly identifies, develops, and delivers advanced capabilities for Special Operations Forces and General Purpose Forces to improve the capacity of the DoD to combat terrorism and irregular

---

[1]Applicable policy guidance includes Presidential National Security Strategy, Defense Strategic Guidance, and any guidance or instructions issued by the ASD (SO/LIC).

adversaries. Second, CTTSO collaborates with and supports related requirements of non-DoD U.S. government agencies and state/local/tribal governments to understand those users' priorities and requirements to share expertise and to develop mutually beneficial capabilities. Third, CTTSO works with partner country ministries of defense under bilateral arrangements to conduct cooperative research and development, which allows the U.S. DoD to leverage foreign experience, expertise, and resources in the fight against terrorists and their infrastructure.

A Unified Goal

International cooperation allows CTTSO to leverage foreign experience, expertise, resources, and infrastructure in a unified approach against terrorism for the benefit of all. Therefore, in addition to its domestic interagency efforts, CTTSO directly manages bilateral agreements with five partner countries (Australia, Canada, Israel, Singapore, and the United Kingdom) and cooperates when appropriate with countries and organizations around the world. Dozens of operational capabilities developed with CTTSO partners are currently in service with a variety of personnel both throughout the United States and around the world.

TECHNICAL
SUPPORT
WORKING GROUP

History and Mission

In April 1982, the National Security Decision Directive 30 assigned responsibility for the development of an overall U.S. policy on terrorism to the Interdepartmental Group on Terrorism (IG/T), chaired by the Department of State (DOS). TSWG was an original subgroup of the IG/T, which later became the Interagency Working Group on Counterterrorism (IWG/CT). In its February 1986 report, a cabinet level Task Force on Counterterrorism – led by then Vice-President Bush – cited TSWG as assuring "the development of appropriate counterterrorism technological efforts."

Today, TSWG still performs that counterterrorism technology development function as a stand-alone interagency working group. TSWG's mission is to identify and prioritize the needs of the national interagency community through research and development programs for combating terrorism requirements. TSWG delivers capabilities to those on the front lines through rapid research and development, testing, and evaluation, while providing operational support. TSWG incorporates available expertise and experience from government, commercial, private, and academic sources throughout the United States and the world.

TSWG initiates efforts to influence longer-term research and development initiatives and balances its technology and capability development efforts among the four pillars of combating terrorism: antiterrorism, counterterrorism, intelligence support, and consequence management.

Organization and Structure

TSWG operates under the policy oversight of the Department of State Coordinator for Counterterrorism and the management and technical oversight of the Department of Defense Assistant Secretary of Defense for Special Operations and Low-Intensity Conflict. TSWG's core funds are derived principally from the Department of Defense and the Department of State, while other departments and agencies contribute additional funds and provide personnel to act as project managers and technical advisors. TSWG has successfully transitioned capabilities to the Departments of Agriculture, Defense, Homeland Security, Justice, State, and Treasury; the Public Health Service; and many other departments

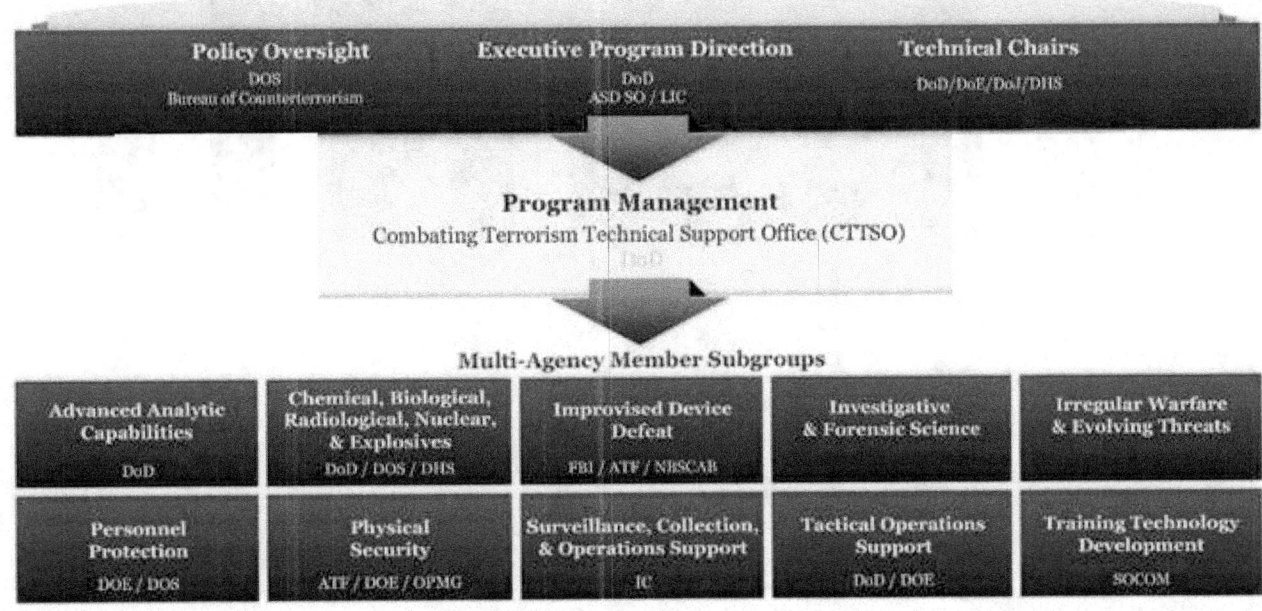

and agencies. Additionally, TSWG has transitioned many systems to state and local law enforcement. TSWG membership includes representatives from more than 100 government organizations. Participation is open not only to federal departments and agencies, but also to first responders and appropriate representatives from state and local governments and international agencies. These departments and agencies work together by participating in one or more subgroups. A comprehensive listing of member organizations is provided in the appendix.

TSWG's subgroups are chaired by senior representatives from DoD and other federal agencies with special expertise in those functional areas. Chairmanship of 10 subgroups is shared as indicated in the organizational chart on the opposite page. Irregular Warfare and Evolving Threats is a new subgroup that was added in fiscal year 14.

TSWG Fiscal Year 2013 Project Funding ($123.7M)

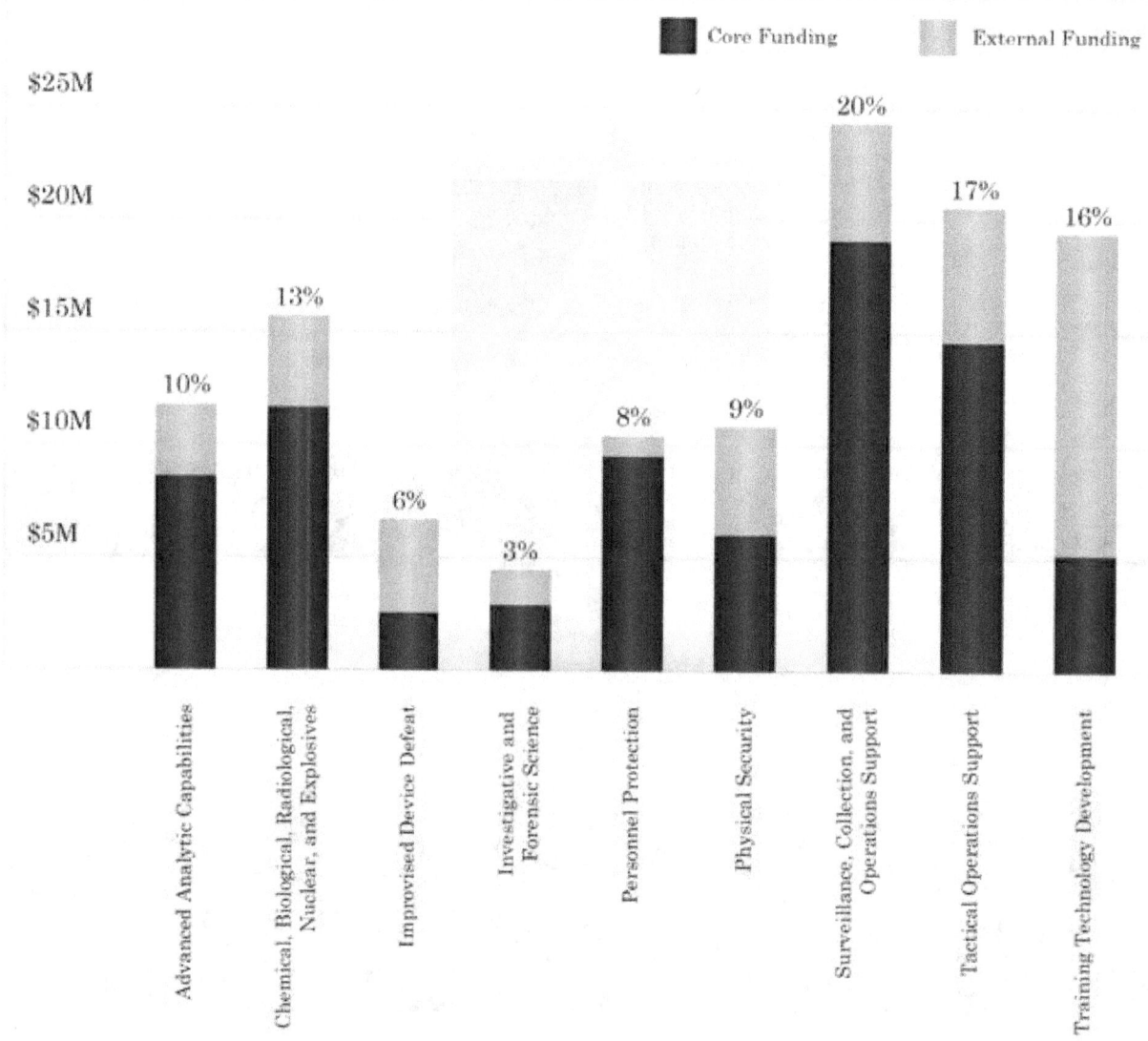

ADVANCED ANALYTIC CAPABILITIES

Mission

Identify, prioritize, and execute research and development projects that satisfy interagency requirements to improve sense making, decision making, and data management for counterterrorism, counterinsurgency, stabilization/re-construction missions, and cyber defense. Focus on the development and integration of analytic tools and associated processes at the tactical level to include operational level interface and user-friendly capabilities that enable better and faster decisions.

aacsubgroup@cttso.gov

Focus Areas

Cyber Defense Applications

Support sustained operations through development and fielding of enhanced layered defensive capabilities by anticipating and avoiding threats through understanding the cyber situation, anticipating adversarial actions, assessing potential impacts, and by implementing defensive methodologies in deployed systems.

Decision, Planning, and Analytical Tools

Develop tools and models that provide analytic rigor to the military and interagency planning and decision making process for counterinsurgency and counterterrorism operations and campaigns. This includes decision support tools that will enable operators and planners at the operational and tactical levels to better understand the operational environment, evaluate first and higher order effects of alternate courses of action, and enable near real-time decisions within the context of the mission.

Integrated Analytic Platforms

Develop and deploy robust integrated platforms to enhance analysis of diverse and disparate data sources to support decision making and planning. These platforms shall enable a variety of analytic tools and methods to be readily interoperable with each other and with supporting data sources. Integrate analytic tools into existing military operational platforms, both forward deployed and reachback capabilities, to facilitate the appropriate interaction, exploration, and visualization of key elements. Develop infrastructure to facilitate secure collaboration and fusion among and between analysts and forward deployed operators in real time.

Stability Operations

Integrate and deploy analytic tools and integrated analytic platforms that support the analyses, operations, and monitoring of stability (and precursors of instability) related to combating terrorism as well as related components of counterinsurgency, law enforcement, and humanitarian assistance and disaster relief. This focus area addresses integrated technology applications that primarily address non-kinetic aspects; decomposing current situations and trends that require dynamic analyses that encompass strategic, operational, and tactical situations; identify potential courses of action (and their higher order effects); identify and monitor measures of effectiveness; identify redlines and tipping points; and adapt to changes on the ground.

Cyber Defense Applications

Network Vulnerability Assessment and Risk Management Strategy for a Smart Grid

Current

Smart Grid is an emerging complex system incorporating power grid, computing, sensing, and communication technologies as well as social interactions to achieve safe, reliable, and efficient electrical energy generation from diverse distributed sources. Smart Grid differs from the legacy electrical grid in the centrality and dependence on sensing, communications, and computing. Pilot Smart Grid installations are being built in several countries around the world, including the United States and Australia.

These range in sophistication from the installation of smart meters to fully integrated Smart Grid networks. The expectation is that Smart Grid deployments will dramatically expand in scale and sophistication in the next decade. Being a critical infrastructure, the security of Smart Grid information systems is clearly of the utmost importance for reliability and safety. The integration of distributed generation resources of diverse types and changes to the distribution grid also pose unique physical security challenges. Everything interacts with everything at the speed of light. The Smart Grid can only be implemented by deeply integrating the power grid and the information and communication technology (ICT) network, which includes high speed broadband. The behaviors of the Smart Grid will be significantly different from the legacy power grid or ICT network alone due to their complex interactions.

This project will provide the much needed techniques and tools for Smart Grid security assessment and enhancement. The research output will serve as an important analysis and decision making tool to assist in safeguarding Smart Grids as one of the critical infrastructure networks. The methodologies can also be applicable in other critical infrastructure complex networks.

Decision, Planning, and Analytical Tools

Sociocultural Awareness through Passive Sensing

Completed

Modern operations have underscored the need for social cultural intelligence in stabilization/reconstruction, counterterrorism, and counterinsurgency missions, particularly in austere and denied areas of operations. Currently available sensor systems and automated analysis tools are optimized for kinetic operations, while manual observations of social cultural intelligence place forces in harm's way. Manual observation is also subject to biases in human observation and judgment. As a result, social cultural intelligence often

several improvements to the base S-CAPS system, which included augmentations to allow for multiple sensor suites, practically-oriented views such as a geospatial view (which allows for labeling and diagramming the collection environment), and the ability to link these views and sensors to the existing S-CAPS social cultural model.

goes unexploited. The Sociocultural Awareness from Passive Sensing (S-CAPS) system addresses this issue by repurposing traditional ISR assets, especially ground sensors, to assess patterns of life, establish baselines for atmospherics, and monitor trends. During the first phase of this project, the system effectively demonstrated the collection of video data and processing social cultural "atmospherics", showing its ability to recognize anomalous activity and pattern of life shifts.

During the second phase of the project, a deployable version of this novel enabling technology employed in SOCOM's Media Production Center focuses on integration with the Susceptibility and Vulnerability Analysis Network Tool (SAVANT), a workflow tool for influence operations. This integration provided a seamless and beneficial capability for military information support operations operators. The integration with the SAVANT suite also brought about

Social Network Analysis Platform

Current

Social Network Analysis Platform (SNAP) is a situational analysis and discovery tool capable of rapidly analyzing streams of unstructured data including classified documents, the Web, and social media. Applicable to irregular warfare and rapidly developing situations, SNAP assists analysts and commanders with assimilating the most relevant and actionable information. The system facilitates speedy and effective planning, preparation, and support of missions. SNAP is built around the Sintelix system, which gathers data, extracts information, and forms networks. Users experience a powerful data exploration environment equipped with network visualization, hyperlink-enhanced source documents, interactive dashboards, and richly featured semantic search.

Continuous Adaptive Improvement of Intelligence Analytics

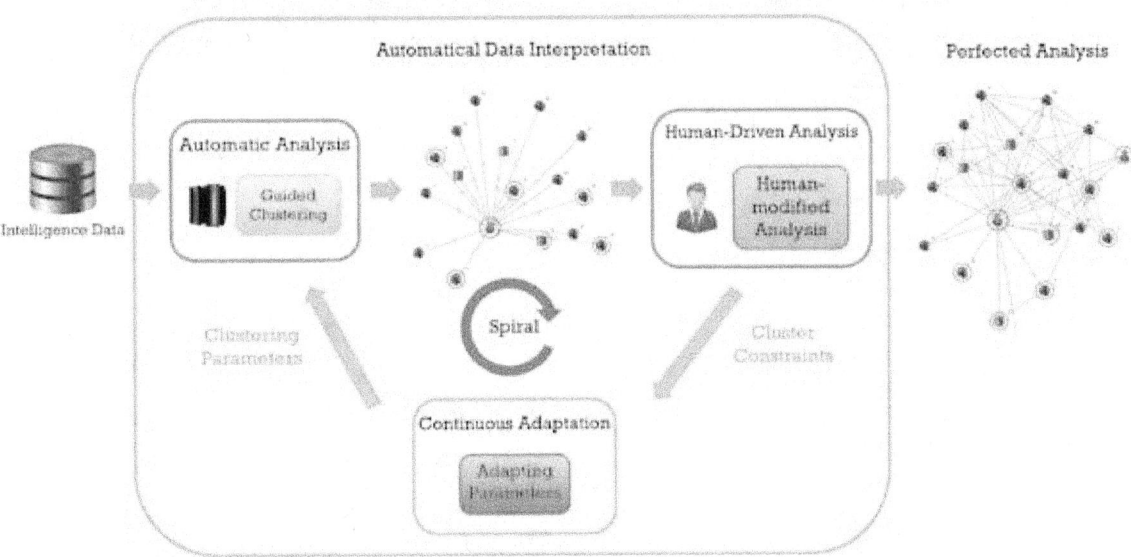

The key technical innovation within SNAP is its ability to continuously improve the automatic analysis it provides. Intelligence processing is accelerated by SNAP's ability to create networks automatically using parametric clustering. SNAP works cooperatively with the analyst in a continuous improvement spiral. It uses guided clustering algorithms iteratively to create entity networks by analyzing incoming documents to resolve entities, track discussion topics, and recognize community structure. Networks are improved in iterative spirals where the analyst makes local refinements, and SNAP generalizes them to the entire network. During a spiral, SNAP progressively returns the network refinements to the continuous learning system, which continuously optimizes the parameters of the parametric clustering algorithm. This improves automatic network creation from incoming data and propagates refinements throughout the existing network.

When complete, SNAP will be able to identify the key players and groups in a situation – their roles, relationships, power bases, and capabilities. From that understanding, it will generate alarms and warnings. SNAP's performance is currently being assessed in real world situations in a collaborative international project.

Integrated Analytic Platforms

Integrated Fusion and Analysis Platform

Completed

Commanders and warfighters on the ground lacked near-term situational awareness of highly complex and dynamic counterinsurgency campaigns.

Palantir was competitively selected to integrate multi-source intelligence in support of advanced analysis, high-level strategic and operational planning, and tactical decision making. As a commercially developed software platform, Palantir is now deployed at many of the most critical intelligence, defense, law enforcement, cyber security, regulation and oversight, humanitarian, and finance missions around the world. By fusing all relevant databases into a single environment, Palantir allows even nontechnical users to easily view, analyze, and share intelligence.

To support warfighters in theater, Palantir deployed disconnected laptops at the tactical edge of the battlefield, regional nodes, and reachback for intelligence support at forward operating bases and in the continental United States. Using Palantir, analysts and warfighters collaborated in real time, ensuring comprehensive situational awareness at all echelons.

Palantir engineers worked with organizations across the DoD through CTTSO to develop custom analytical capabilities to support users in Afghanistan, Iraq, the Horn of Africa, and beyond – helping intelligence analysts manage key leader engagements and kinetic operations, dismantle improvised explosive device networks, and monitor political hotspots in near real time using social media data.

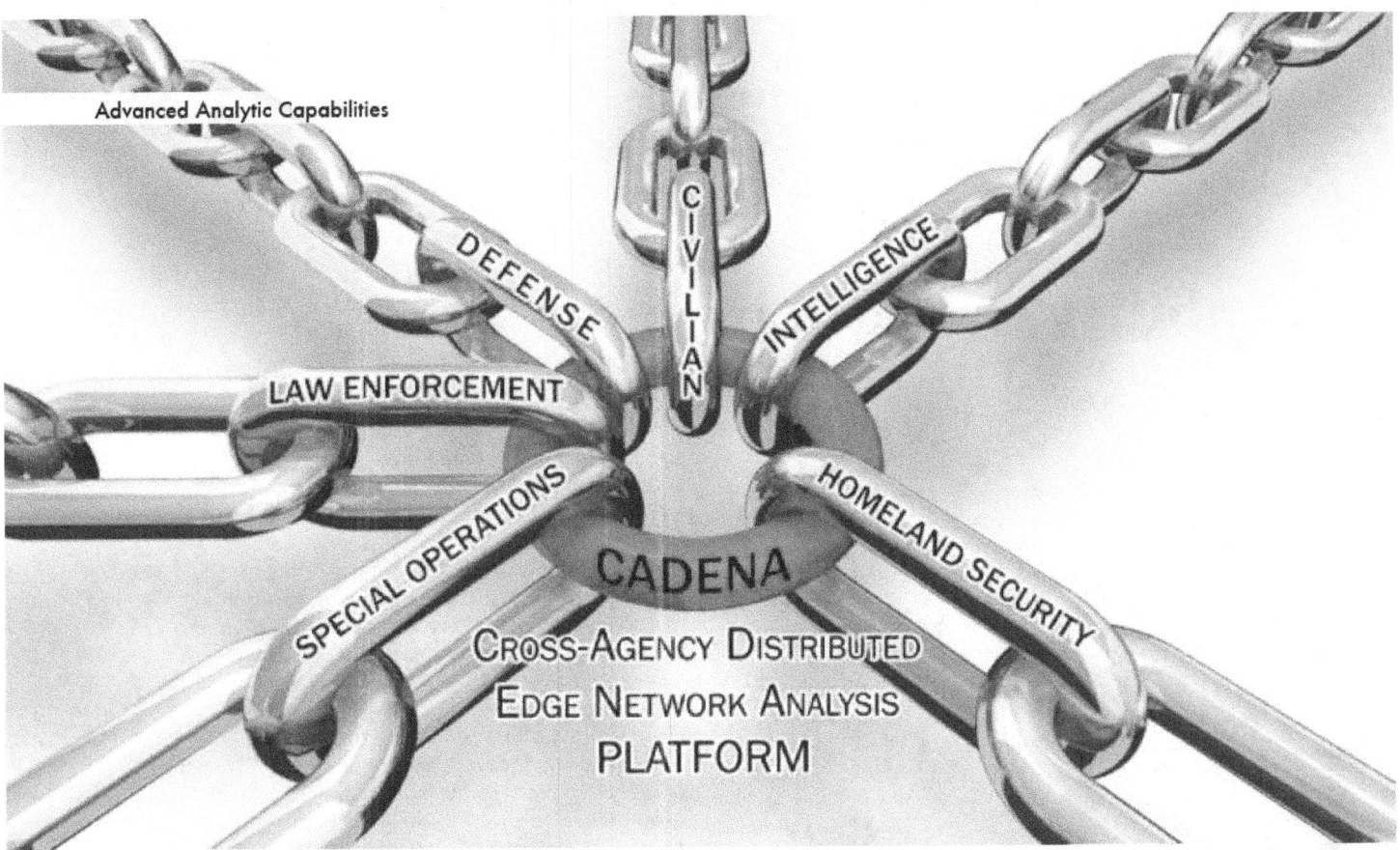

Cross-Agency Distributed Edge Network Analytic Platform

Current

The Cross-Agency Distributed Edge Network Analysis (CADENA) Platform is a suite of existing and proven integrated commercial-off-the-shelf and government-off-the-shelf capabilities designed to be agilely and adaptably employed in support of the interagency mission(s) relevant to the Southwest Border and Puerto Rico. A specific CADENA outcome is reducing the time penalty between the occurrence of events, analysis, decision, and exploitation of opportunity. CADENA provides the capacity to bridge technical and procedural gaps – from the field agent or sensor all the way to the political decision makers. Once deployed, CADENA will provide a tailored capability to each federal agency's requirements so as to augment and integrate with their own existing capabilities and, when permissible, share specific or general information in a secure collaborative analytic environment with other agencies, departments, and law enforcement organizations.

Using mobile apps and leveraging available commercial devices and infrastructure, CADENA can securely equip interagency or intra-agency agents and officers with real-time reporting, Blue Force Tracking (BFT) (when applicable/permissible), data/operational/BFT visualization and situational awareness, as well as real-time reachback collaborative visualization, chat, and data/media exchange with supporting analysts and decision makers and other field elements. The CADENA Platform can integrate this data with existing interagency or intra-agency data sets and feeds and render it in a broad range of analytical and visualization toolsets available within the system including link-nodal, geospatial, temporal, graphical, and others. These tools can be used collaboratively within the integrated workspace as required/permitted according to stakeholder/user authorities and permissions. CADENA also includes a social network analysis methodology and toolset developed by the Naval Postgraduate School CORE lab.

Stability Operations

Model Predictive Controller

Current

The Advanced Analytic Capabilities Subgroup is continuing its efforts in the area of Diplomatic, Information, Military, and Economic/Political, Military, Economic, Social, Information, and Infrastructure campaign planning and execution. The focal point of this work is Model Predictive Control (MPC), a well-grounded engineering discipline that, if properly leveraged, can significantly enhance a system's effectiveness, efficiency, and responsiveness. Work to date has concentrated on defining the MPC's region of applicability within the overall planning and execution domain, and in assessing its potential to add value.

As the role and potential of MPC has become better defined, the effort has begun shifting attention to the practical problems of operationalization. To this end, the effort is currently engaging in real-world studies throughout the operations and intelligence communities – studies currently involving combatant commands, the Department of State, and the Office of the Secretary of Defense's strategic multilevel assessment activity. A second area of attention revolves around current gaps in data access and collaboration infrastructures. Some models demand more data than is currently available and, in turn, require new data collection, new analytical tools and methods, and new interfaces within the planning community. This effort is expected to heavily leverage the Advanced Analytic Capabilities Subgroup's work in this area—in particular, efforts relating to pattern and trend detection and to "fusion-focused" intelligence, surveillance, and reconnaissance collection. A third problem area entails co-evolving MPC and the protocols needed to support operational timelines. Ongoing efforts to get inside the adversary's decision cycle have reduced these timelines from days to hours, or even minutes. The operational challenge does not end there. The effort must ultimately delve into all elements of doctrine, organization, training material, leadership and education, personnel, and facilities.

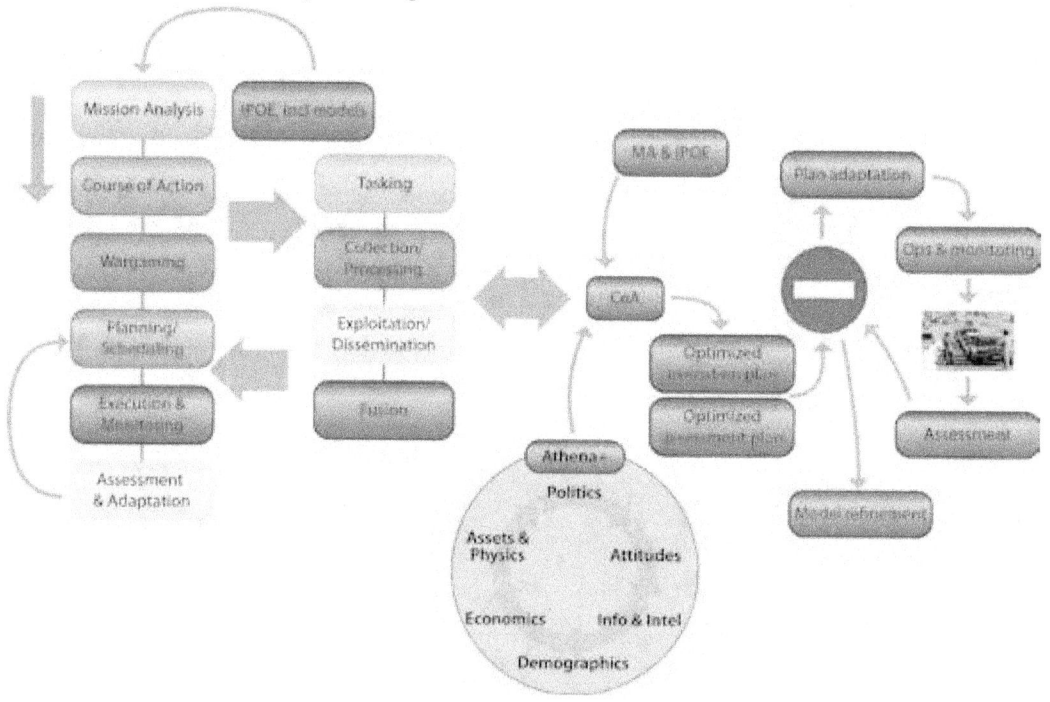

Evidence-Based Planning, Monitoring, and Evaluation

Current

In early fiscal year (FY) 12, the Assistant Commanding General for Police Development, NATO Training Mission - Afghanistan (NTM-A) made a request to the Advanced Analytic Capabilities Subgroup for automated support to their planning, monitoring, and evaluation requirements. In response, the AAC Subgroup sponsored an FY12 and a second FY13 NTM-A pilot of the Evidence-Based Planning, Monitoring, and Evaluation (EPME) system (formerly the Planning, Monitoring, and Evaluation System, or PMES) – a U.S. Army Corps of Engineers developed decision support system. The EPME team provides subject matter expertise and software support to NTM-A. Currently, the EPME team works virtually with select Afghani Ministry of Interior advisor teams to conduct in-depth reviews and monitor the progress of high-priority ministerial development plans (MDP) as preparations for the FY14 transition continue. The reachback support has prototyped multiple modifications to the MDP process and improved reporting formats. The result is a deepened understanding of the critical tasks that still remain, improved ability to advise the Afghan counterparts, and improved monitoring of their progress. The EPME team is also testing applicability of the software in support of interagency and combatant command efforts. These tests are focused on exploiting conflict assessment data and creating structured theory of change visual maps that support stakeholder vetting of assumptions and consensus building on solution options, while accounting for capacity development and shaping activities already in progress on the ground.

EPME is an advanced collaborative methodology to deconstruct the complex problem space of multi-stakeholder operations while developing a common understanding of the key issues to resolve and their causes. It forces testing of known facts and assumptions (evidenced-based). Using the data created in the problem analysis,

it then guides users toward development of solution options suitable for the multiple stakeholders. The end products are traceable and transparent theories of change that explicitly link desired outcomes to intervention activities. The methodology also develops output and outcome indicators that are used to monitor and evaluate progress of the individual activities and the overall outcomes. EPME is enabled by two software tools, the Linking Outputs to Outcome Model (LOOM) and the Metrics Progress Analysis Engine (MPAE). Both tools were developed using Office of the Secretary of Defense small business innovation research funds. LOOM provides a "boundless canvas" that enables the reuse of data developed in the problem analysis to develop desired outcomes and visual representations of the theories of change. As indicators are developed, they are captured and organized in LOOM. LOOM supplies a detailed monitoring and evaluation framework to MPAE including key elements to focus data collection efforts and support data prioritization and indicator parameterization. MPAE provides advanced analytical and visualization capabilities of indicator data, which improves advanced analytical and visualization capabilities of indicator data, which improves the ability to monitor and evaluate the results of intervention activities. The pilots exposed numerous opportunities to refine EPME and the software, resulting in a series of software enhancements now in progress.

CHEMICAL, BIOLOGICAL, RADIOLOGICAL, NUCLEAR, AND EXPLOSIVES

Mission

Identify, prioritize, and execute research and development projects that satisfy the needs of the interagency combating terrorism community to counter the employment of chemical, biological, radiological, nuclear, and explosive materials. Deliver capabilities to the community through rapid research, development, test, and evaluation.

The Chemical, Biological, Radiological, Nuclear, and Explosives (CBRNE) Subgroup identifies and prioritizes multiagency user requirements and competitively seeks technological solutions for countering the terrorist employment of CBRNE materials. Through its participation in the InterAgency Board for Equipment Standardization and Interoperability, and in coordination with the Department of Homeland Security, the National Institutes of Justice, the Environmental Protection Agency, and other Department of Defense components, the CBRNE Subgroup integrates technology requirements from the military, fire, hazardous materials, explosives detection, law enforcement, and emergency medical services communities into its process.

cbrnesubgroup@cttso.gov

Focus Areas

Threat Characterization and Attribution

Investigate the unique physical and chemical characteristics of threat materials, develop tools to determine the origin of a piece of CBRNE evidence, evaluate clandestine methods of CBRNE production, and assess the effects of decontamination on CBRNE evidence.

Consequence Management

Develop equipment to counter the intentional and unintentional releases of CBRNE materials, to include decontamination and restoration.

Information Resources

Integrate shared information management tools to provide on-scene situational awareness.

Protection

Operationally enhance individual and collective protection performance while reducing cost. Develop decision support tools to allow operators to make protective equipment decisions based on field-generated physiological data.

Trace Detection

Develop enabling technologies to detect threat materials and their precursors at trace levels.

Bulk Detection

Develop enabling technologies to detect threat materials and their precursors at bulk levels.

Proximity and Standoff Detection

Develop enabling technologies to detect threat materials and their precursors at proximity and standoff distances.

U.S. Air Force photo/Staff Sgt. Craig Cisek

Threat Characterization and Attribution

BioID

Current

The U.S. government collects and curates a significant amount of genetic, phenotypic, and experimental information on pathogens that may reflect military operations, U.S. forces, or human populations around the world. Ready and effective access to these data sets is a prerequisite to understanding a pathogen's potential impact and formulating successful detection and elimination or mitigation strategies. Historically, these data are generated and analyzed by different laboratories and research teams and stored by those teams in disparate manners and locations. It is problematic for scientists, government officials, and other stakeholders to access, exploit, and correlate pathogen data for decision making, detection, forensics, and gathering signatures and sequences for detection or medical countermeasures.

Unconventional Concepts, Inc. is developing the BioID System to improve access to, sharing, and timely reporting of critical pathogen data by bringing together a pathogen's relevant data in a semantically enhanced, cloud-based

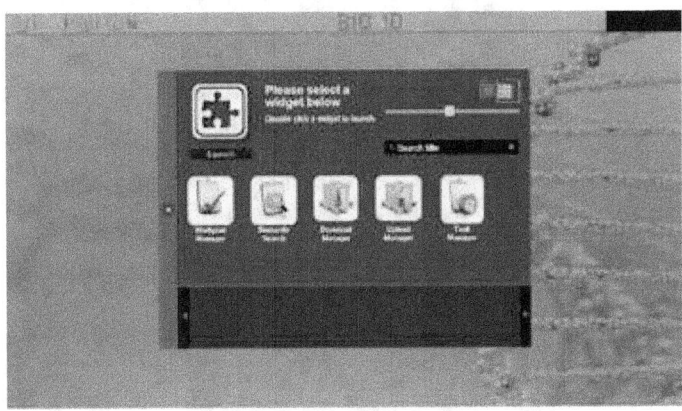

knowledge repository. In addition, BioID will support the laboratory and research teams' pipeline processes; connection to existing documents, spreadsheets, and databases to minimize data entry burden; and quality control and management needs. Pathogen, quality control, and pipeline management data is now accessible via a cloud-based knowledge repository. BioID delivers relevant semantic results for accelerated analysis and intelligent report generation. BioID has reached initial operating capability and is undergoing beta testing.

Information Resources

Technical Workshop and Capability Exercise

Completed

Internationally coordinated and focused research and development (R&D) is essential in order to leverage technical and fiscal resources in combating terrorism. Through three Memorandums of Understanding, CTTSO has involved four partnering nations

in a Quadrilateral (Quad) terms of reference encompassing counterterrorism research and

development. The Technical Response Group (TRG) is one of the international working groups operating under the auspices of the Quad. The TRG meets annually to identify common research and development gaps and initiate research and development projects that improve the capabilities of military and civilian first responders in handling chemical-biological terrorist events. The TRG conducts a Technical Workshop and Capability Exercise (CAPEX) on an alternating annual basis. The CAPEX is a full-scale operational exercise involving technical response teams and equipment from all four countries. Each CAPEX has a unique objective to identify potential equipment and procedureal solutions to first responder issues identified at the workshops. Through the Technical Workshop and CAPEX, the TRG has achieved great success in bringing together military, civilian, emergency responder, and scientific communities to harmonize interface options, share equipment knowledge, and establish protocol solutions to common problems.

CAPEX 2013 was developed to drive research and development requirements for chemical, biological, and radiological (CBR) response capabilities and to share technical and forensic response procedures among the four nations that make up the Quadrilateral Group. Exercise First Landing, conducted April 8-12, 2013, at Joint Expeditionary Base Little Creek-Fort Story in the Commonwealth of Virginia, was the sixth such CAPEX. The exercise consisted of a technical capability demonstration day on April 8 and capabilities scenarios April 9-12. Each individual scenario focused on a CBR incident and provided the participants with a realistic opportunity to demonstrate their capabilities in science, technology, intelligence and law enforcement, technical response, and consequence management as they relate to CBR terrorism. These capabilities provided the foundation for the team objectives, around which the scenarios were built, to include a chemical lab disguised as narcoterrorism, a biological lab producing a nontraditional biological agent, and an attempted radiological attack using special nuclear material.

Green Field III

Completed

The objectives of the Green Field Program were to measure radiation contamination levels on the ground and the radioactive particle concentration in the air, downwind from the detonation point, and to compare the results expected using the Green Field Model. Three series of Green Field (GF) experiments have been completed to date. GFI evaluated the cloud rise model for realistic radiological dispersion device (RDD) threat weights, and from the data obtained, incorporated new source terms into Hot Spot and LODI models. GFII evaluated "ground zero" characteristics, explosive aerosolization, and dispersion patterns. Data obtained from GFII was used to refine models for areas of particular interest to first responders and to drive clean-up planning after an RDD event.

GFIII studied the situations where radioactive material is dispersed to the atmosphere by explosives. This was completed through the inclusion of different measuring systems, different ground surfaces, and different device geometries compared to the previous phase of the project (GFII). The objectives of GFIII were to develop guidelines for both first responders and the environmental protection teams during the early and later phases following an RDD terrorism event. Revised parameters were formulated by comparing results obtained from GFIII to those predicted by existing dispersion models used for risk assessment.

Protection

Flexible PAPR

Current

The current approach to CBRN respiratory protection has forced the operator to select a certified respirator to operate in a known threat scenario. Time necessary to respond to an incident commonly exceeds available respiratory protection capabilities. The use of a CBRN low profile powered air purifying respirator (PAPR) that is able to be configured as a combination respirator unit extends wear duration significantly with less user burden. However, PAPRs cannot be used in unknown or high risk environments. Therefore, a number of performance tradeoffs have been accepted within the specialist community, leading to a less than optimum tactical approach to missions with increased user risk.

Avon Protection Systems Inc. is developing a low-profile PAPR module for use with existing self-contained breathing apparatus (SCBA) units and a modular hose – a universal hose that connects the mask, PAPR, and SCBA, therefore reducing the number of hoses required from two to one. The modular hose was previously designed for CTTSO and provides the capability to operate 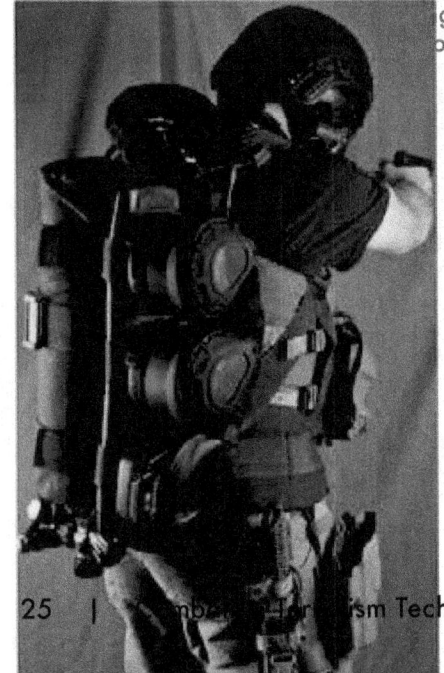 g a lightweight ombination system. This new design provides the user with a system that addresses the past safety considerations in a user-friendly, lightweight design. The new system will be certified to all applicable National Institute for Occupational Safety and Health and National Fire Protection Association CBRN standards.

Next Generation CB Glove

Current

AirBoss Defense is developing a next generation chemical and biological (CB) glove that provides National Fire Protection Association (NFPA) 1994, Class 3 protection while providing greater tactility, durability, dexterity, and comfort over the traditional butyl glove. The current generation butyl rubber CB gloves lack breathability and have poor heat and moisture management, which causes thermal discomfort to the user.

The new AirBoss glove will significantly reduce the thermal burden and allow the user to meet their operational demands by improving dexterity while still providing extended mission percutaneous protection from exposure to the harmful effects of all traditional CB warfare agents and the toxic industrial chemicals listed in NFPA 1994.

Improved Liquid Tight Integrity Testing

Current

International Personnel Protection (IPP) is developing new procedures that will improve how barrier protective clothing for first responders is evaluated to limit exposure to hazardous liquids. The current approach for measuring liquid integrity of protective clothing and ensembles is embodied in the American Society for Testing and Materials F1359, Standard Test Method for Liquid Penetration Resistance of Protective Clothing or Protective Ensembles under a Shower Spray While on a Mannequin. Currently, this test is specified in nearly every barrier clothing standard for first responders, including those of the National Fire Protection Association and National Institute of Justice.

The "shower" test, as it has commonly been called, has focused attention on garment design, particularly for closures and interfaces with other clothing items, but has also been criticized for being overly rigorous, lacking consistency, and making it difficult to identify failure modes. The IPP effort will develop sensors to replace the

subjective determinations of liquid penetration made as part of the test. In addition, this effort will address current deficiencies in existing test protocols for measuring liquid integrity of protective clothing and ensembles, including reproducibility, realistic field exposures, and manikin standardization. Additionally, the test method will be validated through inter-laboratory testing, and the proposed changes will be sent for review to the appropriate development standards committees.

Trace Detection

Single Detector for Chemical Warfare Agents and Toxic Industrial Chemicals

Completed

Detection and identification of chemical threats is a continuing problem for military, security, and emergency responder personnel. Emergency response teams carry a variety of pieces of detection equipment to measure chemical warfare agents and toxic industrial chemicals (TIC). In an effort to streamline operations and reduce overall cost, teams require a single detector to meet the varied detection needs. A capability gap was identified for an

orthogonal detector system that uses multiple techniques that measure properties that are not closely related (e.g., photoionization and infrared spectroscopy) to achieve overall detection performance.

Thermo Fisher Scientific developed a single detector with the capability of providing a secondary confirmation for chemical identification based upon orthogonal detection techniques. The rugged system is field-portable, self-calibrating, battery operated, capable of being decontaminated, and can accurately determine chemical concentrations and be operable within five minutes of set up. This capability will greatly reduce the false positives found in field operations.

The portable, handheld, Orthogonal TIC Detector (OTD) system combines photoionization detection and electrochemical detection with the optical engine based on Thermo Scientific's gas-phase Fourier-transform infrared spectrometer, the TruDefender® FTG for the detection and identification of gases and vapors. The system includes sensors for lower explosive limit and oxygen, a photoionization detector, and six other electrochemical cells. Software on the OTD will use data from all of the detectors to set calibrations and validate the analysis.

Bulk Detection

Dual Wavelength Raman

Completed

Sample fluorescence can interfere with Raman spectra. Sample fluorescence can be greatly reduced by using a longer-wavelength laser for Raman excitation, at the expense of Raman signal. Thermo Fisher Scientific's handheld Raman spectrometer, FirstDefender (FD) uses 785 nm excitation to generate Raman signal from a solid or liquid analyte. In use, the FD collects data until a set signal to noise ratio (SNR) is achieved. A system capable of achieving SNR levels comparable to Thermo Fisher Scientific's FD, but using 1030 nm excitation, would extend the universe of analyzable chemicals considerably, while keeping the same scan times as the FD.

Thermo Fisher Scientific developed a portable, handheld Raman device that utilizes two excitation wavelengths: 785 nm and 1030 nm. The 785 nm portion of the system gives better SNR but causes fluorescence in some materials, while the 1030 nm portion gives less SNR but far less fluorescence. The combination of the two capabilities into a dual-wavelength Raman instrument yields a versatile, high-performance instrument with wide applicability for identification of solids and liquids.

Flash Portal

Completed

Artkis Radiation Detectors Ltd in Switzerland has been at the forefront of developing and testing a sensitive, affordable, reliable, and sustainable new detection system that complements and can be easily integrated in existing detection portal systems for fissionable materials – plutonium and uranium. This technology responds to a pressing worldwide need to provide an alternative to

one of the major existing neutron detector systems. These old systems depend on a man-made isotope of helium, He-3, to detect much lower energy neutrons, also known as thermal neutrons. A very limited supply and a dramatic increase in demand have driven prices of He-3 to unsustainable levels.

FLASH, the Artkis system, is an international collaboration dedicated to improving public security against nuclear threats. FLASH replaces the scarce man-made helium isotope with regular helium, like in party balloons. The regular helium detects the neutrons emitted directly by the fission events of uranium or plutonium nuclei by detecting brief flashes of light that are generated as the fast neutrons transit the regular helium gas.

In independent testing in the United Kingdom and in Italy, the field-ready prototype successfully demonstrated the necessary sensitivity and high reliability. Since fast neutrons come directly from the fissioning nuclei, the neutrons provide valuable directional information pointing to the source. The low energy neutrons start life as high energy fast neutrons but lose their energy through scattering off intervening material that destroy any information about the direction to the source from He-3 detectors. FLASH testing also documented the effectiveness of using fission gamma ray

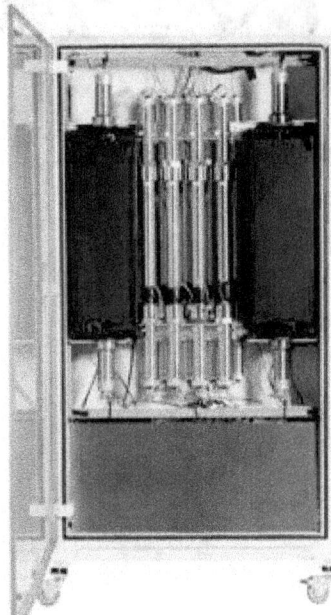

detections to trigger detection time windows for the fast neutrons. This significantly reduced background and improved signal-to-noise, providing greater sensitivity.

Artkis Radiation Detectors Ltd won the 2011 CTTSO-sponsored Global Security Challenge. The CTTSO project integrated significant technical manpower, material, and testing support contributed as part of the international FLASH effort by AWE, the UK Atomic Weapons Establishment, and the European Commission's Joint Research Centre in Italy. The U.S. Department of Homeland Security's Domestic Nuclear Detection Office monitored the progress of the development and testing.

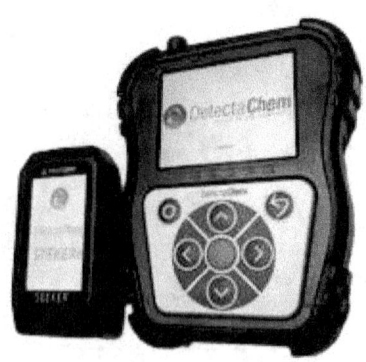

Miniaturization of Automated Colorimetric Test Kit for Explosives Detection

Current

The use of homemade explosives (HME) for use in improvised explosive devices (IEDs) is of great concern to the U.S. military, first responders, law enforcement, and security forces. Terrorist incidents involving HMEs have become a global threat because of the accessibility of explosive recipes in the public domain. To meet the challenge of detecting both military grade and HME-based explosives, a detection kit must provide a broad range of capabilities and characteristics, the capability to detect and identify a wide range of threat materials, ease of use, affordability, reliability, and be easily deployable. Colorimetric detection technology is based upon a series of chemical reactions that produce a visual response, most often in the form of a color, in the presence of certain chemical structures or substances. Traditionally, operators compare the observed response to manufacturer-supplied guidelines in order to confirm the presence and identity of explosive material in the sample. A handheld HME trace detector with automated analysis may provide a reliable, low maintenance, simple device capable of operating in diverse environmental conditions to meet customer needs in the field.

Detectachem, LLC is developing a miniaturized automated colorimetric test kit based on the current SEEKER XDU model (at approx 50 percent of the original sized unit) is being developed. The swipe cards used determine the presence of explosives of interest.

Proximity and Standoff Detection

Raman-Off II

Current

Vehicle-borne improvised explosive devices (VBIEDs) continue to pose a significant threat to U.S. interests at home and abroad. Numerous challenges are associated with detecting VBIEDs. CTTSO and the Department of Homeland Security Science and Technology Directorate (DHS S&T) initiated a multi-phased study to determine the state-of-the-art of optical standoff explsoives detection technologies, as applied to VBIED applications.

When an analyte of interest is subjected to an excitation laser, a fingerprint spectrum, specific to the analyte of interest is generated. Optical spectroscopy is a proven technology and a potential method for remote standoff detection. A laboratory and field feasibility study was conducted to determine the effectiveness of optical spectroscopy as a means of standoff detection.

DHS S&T issued two requests for information (RFI) solications on standoff techniques as they are applied in detecting VBIEDs. Activities in Phase 1 consisted of the publication of an RFI in 2008 and testing that involved the Transportation Security Laboratory shipping trace explosive test articles to developers for analysis at their site. Phase 2 activities included the publication of an RFI in 2009 and further testing with an expanded test matrix. Phase 2 was completed at the developers' facilities by the Transportation Security Laboratory testing team. The general conclusion of this work in broad terms was that any reliable standoff technology for VBIEDs will need to have the detection increased by at least two to three orders of magnitude. This may occur through increasing the power of the probing energy, increasing the power detected, or exploiting processes (as yet unidentified) that would increase overall efficiency.

Since the culmination of Raman-Off I, numerous strides have been made in the advancement of optical standoff explosives detection technologies. An upcoming Phase 3 effort (2013-2014) will provide the next snapshot view of the state of technology that exists today.

IMPROVISED DEVICE DEFEAT

Mission

Identify, prioritize, and execute projects that satisfy mission critical needs and address interagency requirements for advanced technologies to safely and effectively defeat improvised terrorist devices.

The Improvised Device Defeat (IDD) Subgroup delivers advanced technologies, tools, and information to increase the operational capabilities of the U.S. military Explosive Ordnance Disposal (EOD) community and federal, state, and local bomb squads to defeat and neutralize terrorist devices. In collaboration with military, federal, state, and local agencies, the IDD Subgroup identifies and prioritizes multi-agency user requirements through joint working groups and thorough validation processes.

iddsubgroup@cttso.gov

Focus Areas

Device Defeat

Develop advanced technologies to defeat the broad spectrum of improvised terrorist devices, to include IEDs, vehicle-borne improvised explosive devices (VBIEDs), person-borne IEDs (PBIEDs), and enhanced hazard devices containing chemical, biological, or radiological materials. Develop innovative, cost-effective disruption and precision render-safe solutions that increase standoff distance, reduce collateral damage, and decrease risk to the improvised devices defeat operator. Improve neutralization techniques for both sensitive and insensitive explosives and enhanced payloads such as flammable liquids and gases.

Access and Diagnostics

Develop reliable, precise, and cost-effective advanced technical solutions and procedures to improve military and civilian bomb squad technicians' diagnostic analysis of IEDs. Develop and advance technologies that identify and locate the IED, explosive, or enhanced fillers, and key fuzing and firing components. Develop testing methodologies and protocols that define and confirm the access, diagnostic tool, or procedure's ability to satisfy expected design and operational parameters.

Emerging Threats

Advance production of effective countermeasures to neutralize or defeat radio-controlled IEDs and provide safe environments for improvised device defeat operators. Develop, characterize, and test technology solutions to effectively render safe improvised devices using novel fuzing systems that incorporate such items as electronic sensors, microcontrollers, or mechatronic[1] components.

Remote Procedures

Develop advanced application systems to remotely access, diagnose, and defeat improvised devices. Advance development of manufacturer- and model-independent products and robotics with plug and play interface. Develop an open architecture, navigation, communication, and operator controls for robotic platforms, tools, and sensors. Develop advanced application systems to remotely access, diagnose, and defeat improvised devices.

Tool Characterization and Information Resources

Improve performance evaluation methodologies, test procedures, and tool characterization models for improvised device defeat technologies. Conduct ongoing evaluation and improvement of tools, methods, and protocols for confirming the accuracy of detection equipment, reliability of diagnostic tools, and completeness of neutralization and render safe techniques. Advance training concepts and information delivery systems that promote the tactical operational response readiness required to effectively, safely, and efficiently counter improvised devices and emerging threats.

Maritime Security

Develop technologies to protect ships, boats, docking facilities, offshore platforms, shore side loading facilities, power plants, bridges, and marine cables and pipelines from any form of terrorist attack, including water-borne and underwater IEDs. Develop and test technologies to include manned or unmanned long- and short-range sensors for detection and tracking; physical barriers and stopping devices; unmanned surface, underwater, and air vehicles; weapons; armor; life support; diving and underwater systems; and mammal systems.

1-Mechatronics adds intelligence to a mechanical design or replaces a mechanical design with an intelligent electronic solution. An example of a mechatronic component is the digital thermostat, which has replaced the much more inefficient mechanical thermostat. Digital thermostats are more accurate and are typically programmable, allowing for increased efficiency.

Device Defeat

Commercialization of the Scalable Improvised Device Defeat System

Completed

The Scalable Improvised Device Defeat (SIDD) system is an affordable and commercially available explosively-driven water-jet disrupter system that offers tactical flexibility to civilian bomb squads and military EOD technicians. Applied Research Associates, Inc., in conjunction with the Denver Police and Colorado Springs Police Bomb Squads, tested and evaluated the SIDD on different test trials and witnessed the water-jet velocity and penetration energy imparted on the test plates. The SIDD is available in three different sizes – 5, 10, and 15 gallons, giving the bomb technician options on which tool to use depending on the scenario. The SIDD is capable of disrupting the firing train of the IED while minimizing the collateral damage. The SIDD features non-fragmenting, non-metallic construction with ideal geometric dimensions for disruption capability and can be rapidly deployed manually or robotically. The SIDD is available for purchase online at www.araforce.com.

Automatic Wire Cutter

Current

The Automatic Wire Cutter (AWC) provides bomb technicians with a safe and effective reusable tool to non-explosively cut multiple gauge/sized wires. The AWC is a robust, lightweight tool that has a time-delayed cutter, allowing technicians to successfully render safe command-wire-initiated IEDs and trip-wire-actuated devices from a safe distance. The AWC uses a mechanical timer, which can be set to either 30 or 120 seconds, to trigger a spring-driven hammer against a ceramic utility knife blade. In addition to the timed-delay automatic cutting capability, the AWC can also be triggered manually to cut wires. It can be attached to a pull cord to perform remote manual cutting (i.e., without using the timer).

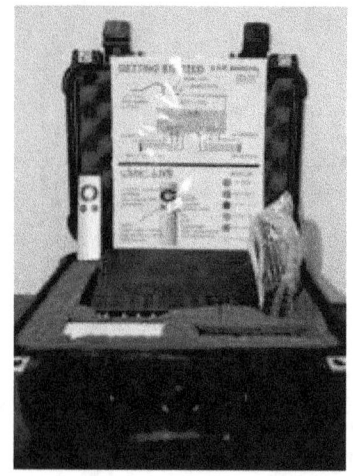

Remote Procedures

iLIVE Video Enhancement System

Completed

The current problem with unmanned ground vehicles' cameras is that their optics are not designed for maximum efficiency in all lighting conditions. The inLine Instant Video Enhancement (iLive) System provides an enhanced viewing capability for camera operators in low light conditions. Using the Lightweight Enhanced Night/Day Vision System software library, the iLIVE system can turn night into day and offer enhanced viewing and targeting for EOD robotics and remote cameras. The iLIVE is compatible with analog or digital video inputs and can deliver the enhanced images to any video display system chosen by the user. The iLIVE's small footprint and power requirements enable mounting to many remotely operated vehicles on sea, land, or air, as well as to fixed camera assets with little to no impact on the performance of the chosen vehicle or system. The iLIVE system leverages existing camera systems using a highly innovative software library implemented on a multimedia digital signal processing chip, giving the user unprecedented viewing, usability, and targeting functions.

iLIVE is a low light camera enhancement with day or night capability using digital signal processor technology for a real-time display. Analog or digital video input/output with standard connections is available. The small size allows for easy mounting on EOD robots with remote controls. Additional information on iLive can be obtained at www.ampware.com.

Tool Characterization and Information Resources

Improvised Explosive Device Instant Notification System

Completed

The Improvised Explosive Device (IED) Instant Notification System (INS) is an application (app) designed to be downloaded onto smartphones (Androids or iPhones) from the Google Play or iTunes stores by every certified Public Safety Bomb Technician and by National Bomb Squad Commanders Advisory Board (NBSCAB) account users. The IED INS app was developed by Applied Research Associates, Incorporated to allow bomb technicians to create, edit, and send messages in real time to other bomb technicians and bomb squads as they're en-route or have arrived at the incident site. The bomb technician can quickly post a message by using his smartphone app drop down menu to select relevant key identification features or components and can then send out an alert to other squads in the area. The responding bomb technician or another technician on his squad can send out updates, request for additional technicians or equipment, or receive information from other squads that have permissions (mutual aid agreements) to respond to the initial post. This app will enable bomb squads to receive incident alerts from all across the country or can be tailored to a specific region or state in which the bomb squad is interested. This app is available on the Google Play store and the iTunes store and is being field tested and evaluated with several bomb squads across the United States.

Bomb Technician Wikipedia

Current

The Bomb Technician Wikipedia (Wiki) is now active on the website of the National Bomb Squad Commander's Advisory Board (NBSCAB) and has already become important as the official site for NBSCAB to post special bomb squad related definitions that are not included in the most recent Weapons Technical Intelligence Lexicon. The Bomb Technician Wiki is only accessible to the approximately 3,000 currently certified public safety bomb technicians since it resides within the NBSCAB website, which is password protected and is updated with new user data from the FBI Hazardous Devices School continuously. The community-driven format of the Bomb Technician Wiki provides state and local bomb squads with an unclassified reference capability that does not exist anywhere else. The Bomb Technician Wiki is servicing the community and providing an easily accessible repository of useful, unclassified information in one place. There are 467 accredited bomb squads in the U.S., diverse in geography and experience. The Bomb Technician Wiki uses industry standard software and was fully launched during November of 2012. The Bomb Technician Wiki is a repository for useful reference material for all accredited bomb technicians and includes a useful mix of references, guides, and definitions covering policy, operational, training equipment, technical, and historical matters.

Southwest Border C-IED Working Group

The U.S.-Mexico border is a highly unique area of operation (AOR) with an environment and trends that are unique and specific to this AOR. The environment and trends are unique and specific to this AOR. Bomb squads along the U.S.-Mexico border require unconventional techniques, training, and equipment that are not needed by most U.S. civilian squads. These factors make equipment and training specific to this AOR a necessity to provide public safety bomb squads and their military and federal partners with the tools they need to safely and effectively address the current issues along the U.S. borders. The Southwest Border C-IED Working Group (SWBCIEDWG) was established with the primary goal to communicate, provide solutions to the unique operating techniques, and identify key issues and needs. Invitees were members of state and local bomb squads that operate along the U.S.-Mexico border and/or have an international port of entry in their AOR. Federal invitees were selected from military and federal law enforcement agencies that provide support to state and local squads meeting the selection criteria. The SWBCIEDWG, in existence only one year, has already made progress solving many action items generated in the first meeting. A model dismount and air operations policy has been authored. Port responses have been discussed and briefed in detail and are now more aligned jurisdiction by jurisdiction along the border. Equipment sets have been identified and are being acquired by the squads, complementing their gear load outs and providing border specific resources, which were previously lacking.

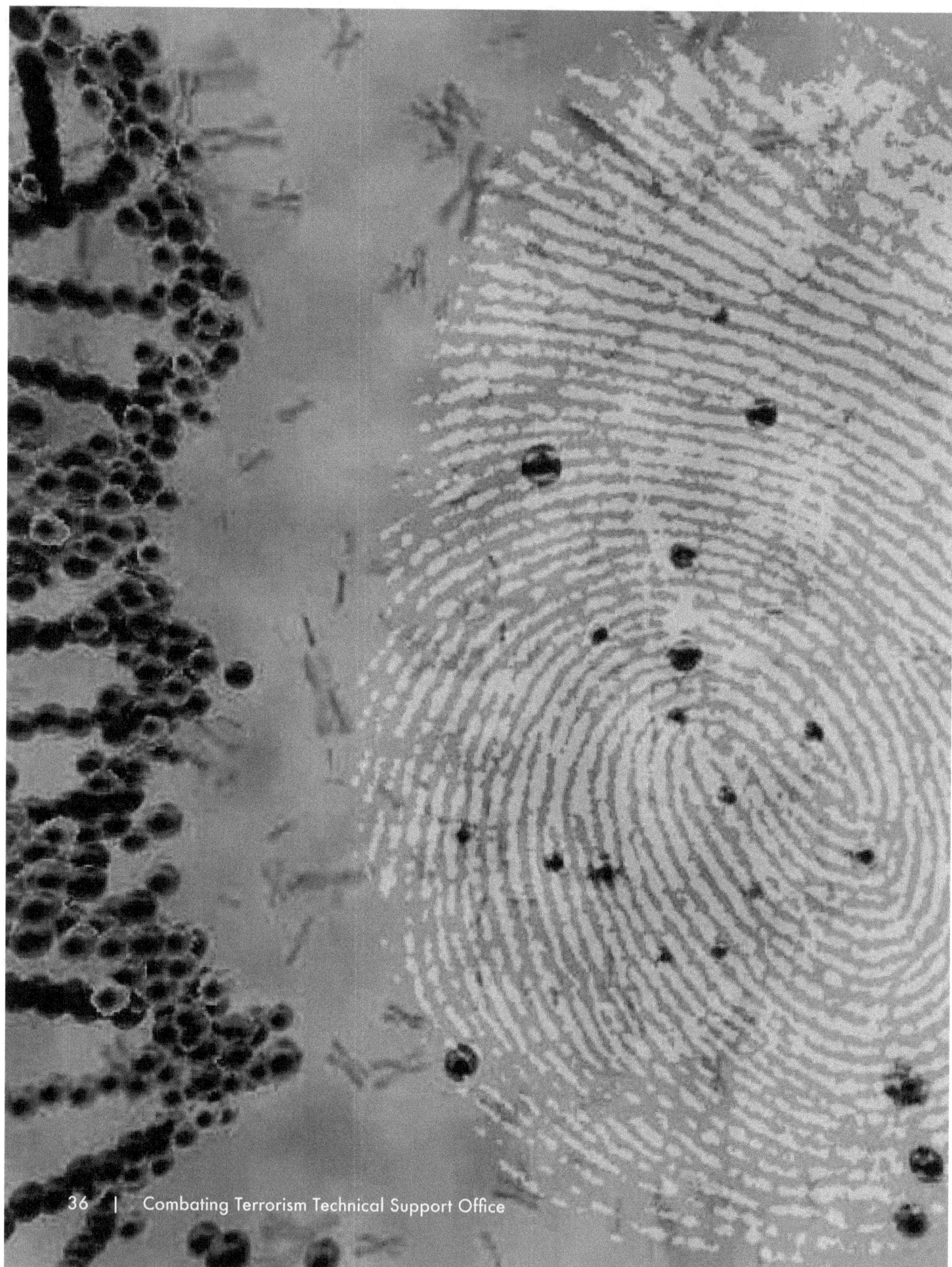

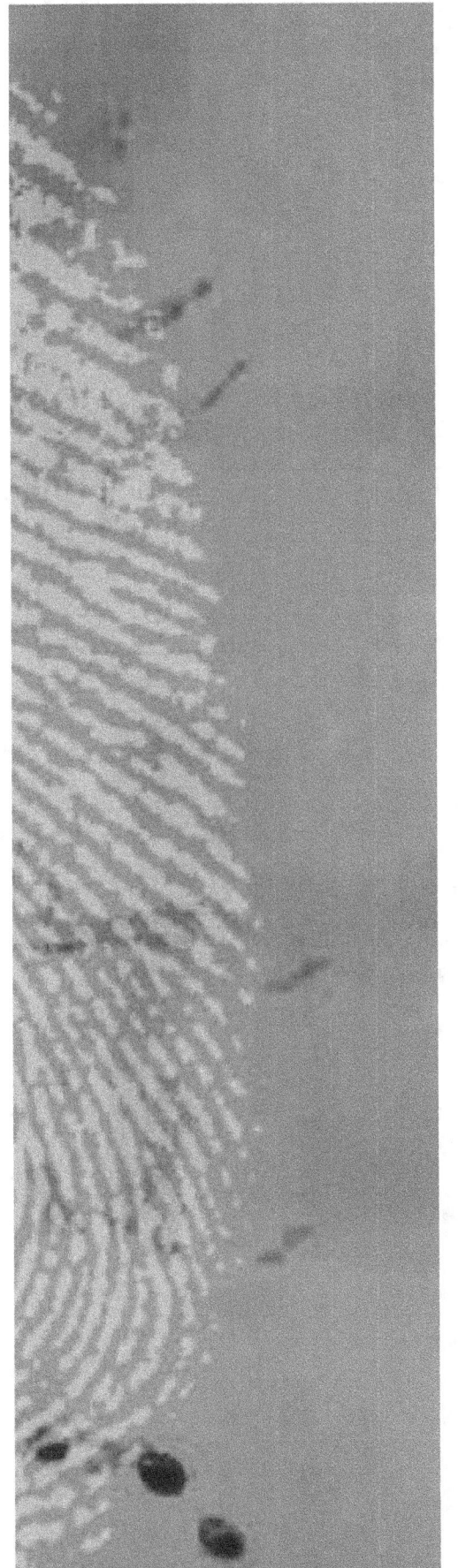

INVESTIGATIVE AND FORENSIC SCIENCE

Mission

Identify, prioritize, and execute research and development projects of multi-agency interest that provide investigative and forensic support to terrorist-related counteraction, investigations, and analysis.

The Investigative and Forensic Science (IFS) Subgroup executes wide-ranging research and development to advance investigative and forensic science. The subgroup focuses on crime scene response, criminalistics, electronic evidence (i.e., multimedia forensics), forensic intelligence, and identity knowledge. IFS works with a diverse group of international, federal interagency, and select state/provincial/municipal law enforcement, investigative, forensic science, and forensic intelligence stakeholders as well as partners in the Department of Defense and intelligence community to produce advanced and new technology and methods that improve mission capabilities for combating terrorism. The subgroup strives to be groundbreaking, relevant to combating terrorism, and vital to the Defense Forensic Enterprise system.

ifssubgroup@cttso.gov

Focus Areas

Crime Scene Response

Improve the quality of recognition, documentation, collection, and preservation of evidence as well as the safety of first responders at a scene. Improve the capability of first responders and forensic examiners to process and record terrorist incident scenes for future prosecution.

Criminalistics

Advance the capability to identify and evaluate physical evidence by the application of physical and natural sciences and technology. Improve the efficiency and speed of the analysis and evaluation of physical evidence and the reporting of results to end users. Develop new and more efficient forensic capabilities.

Electronic Evidence

Develop computer forensic hardware, software, decryption tools, and digital methods to investigate terrorism. Identify computer systems and media used by terrorists and acquire from them the maximum amount of evidence. Develop advanced methods to extract and enhance audio recordings from surveillance sources. Improve techniques for the analysis of electronic devices to obtain the most forensic information.

Forensic Intelligence

Develop advanced multi-disciplinary forensic and scientific techniques to perform sensitive site exploitation and process incident response scenes to acquire, collate, analyze, and disseminate law enforcement and tactical actionable intelligence and information. Develop improved interrogation, interviewing, and credibility assessment methods. Improve related technical surveillance methods.

Identity Knowledge

Develop new scientific technology for the specific identification of individuals who have committed or are associated with terrorist acts. Improve the capability to use physical evidence to individualize or classify subjects or persons of interest.

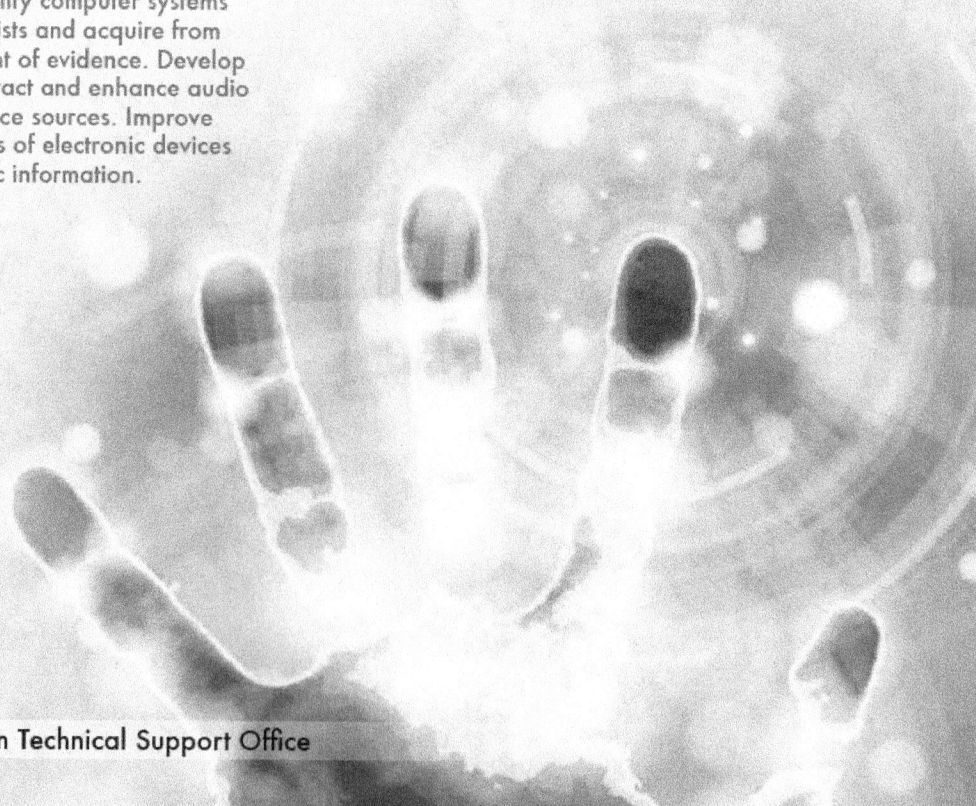

Criminalistics

Thermal Ribbon Analysis Platform

Completed

Fraudulent and counterfeit documents are an essential tool for terrorists and criminals when they engage in many activities such as illegal border crossings, credit card fraud, financial crimes, and unauthorized entry of facilities. When high quality commercial type images are required, the documents are most often produced on printers with thermal ribbons. Any given portion of a thermal ribbon is only used one time, so it retains a latent image of what it printed. Locating these images and synchronizing the images of the different colored ribbons can produce a complete image of what was printed. This will positively identify the specific printer used for a given document as well as determine exactly what was printed when the counterfeit document is unavailable. Quantum Signal LLC developed a hardware-software system that is able to rapidly identify and extract the latent images on thermal ribbons and then reproduce an image of the document or graphics. The system allows for the enhancement of recovered images and tracks the entire forensic process to ensure admissibility in court. The hardware fits on a bench or countertop and requires a minimal amount of training to operate. The final deliverable is an efficient comprehensive tool to identify what printer created a document or image without having to reconstitute the image.

Immunogenic Fingerprint Reagents

Current

New methods are constantly required to push latent print detection limits down to the lowest limits possible. The nature of the investigative and counterterrorism missions of the law enforcement and intelligence communities compels these groups to continue to improve existing technologies or develop new strategies. As terrorist groups have recently adopted asymmetric tactics to inflict horrific damage on people and property, nontraditional strategies to meet these challenges must be adopted. This international project with the Defence Science and Technology Organization in Canberra, Australia, is looking to develop and validate a nontraditional latent fingerprint detection method based on novel antibodies and nano-technology approaches. This project will develop new antigenic reagents targeting other chemicals commonly found in latent fingerprints such as carbohydrates, fatty acids, sterols, and proteins. It will improve the selectivity and sensitivity compared to existing methods and then become compatible with standard laboratory equipment and existing processing sequences.

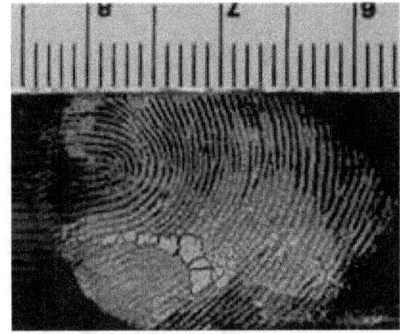

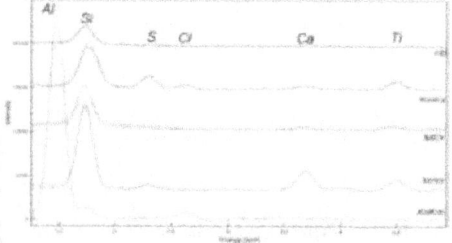

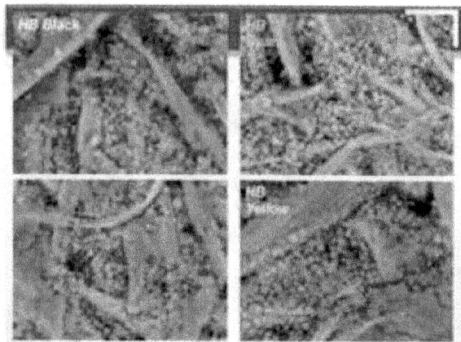

Forensic Ink Analysis and Comparison System

Current

Forensic document analysis makes a significant contribution to identifying terrorists and their networks. Terrorists frequently use fraudulent documents to accomplish their objectives. Analysis of these documents to extract the maximum amount of evidence and intelligence is vital in the fight against the terrorists. Besides providing a wealth of information, the ink in fraudulent documents can link the documents to individual terrorists, their networks, specific incidents, and locations. This project will provide a capability to U.S. forces and law enforcement to link the documents as well as provide other forensic intelligence. Florida International University is developing an automated identification and analysis system for the inks from copiers, inkjet printers, and traditional print ink using multi-discipline scientific techniques based on chemical and physical traits. The system will automatically compare the traits to those in a database to eliminate the ink from others and determine if the documents are counterfeit or genuine.

Comparative Analysis of Material from HMEs and Improvised Explosive Devices

Current

Homemade explosives (HMEs) and improvised explosive devices (IEDs) are still a weapon of choice for terrorists. During investigations of explosions or when unexploded HMEs and IEDs are found, determining the source of the materials used in the HME or IED provides valuable investigative information. Another critical item is to link the HME or IED to other events and to geographic regions. These links are especially critical when other evidence is not available to identify the specific maker or bomber. Isotope ratio determinations have been shown to provide valuable information in several different types of forensic applications and have been employed in some explosive related analysis in the past. They represent a potential to link HMEs and IEDs to events, regions, and sources. This international project with Flinders University in Australia is developing the capability to take materials or residue from HMEs/IEDs and compare it to other HME/IED residue for event-to-event linking and through comparison with a database to identify the most likely geographical origin of the materials from event-to-source and source-to-region. The end state of this project will be a searchable database and map for determining the geographical origin of materials or residues from HMEs/IEDs by comparison of isotopes, ratios, and metals on an event-to-event, event-to-source, and source-to-region scale.

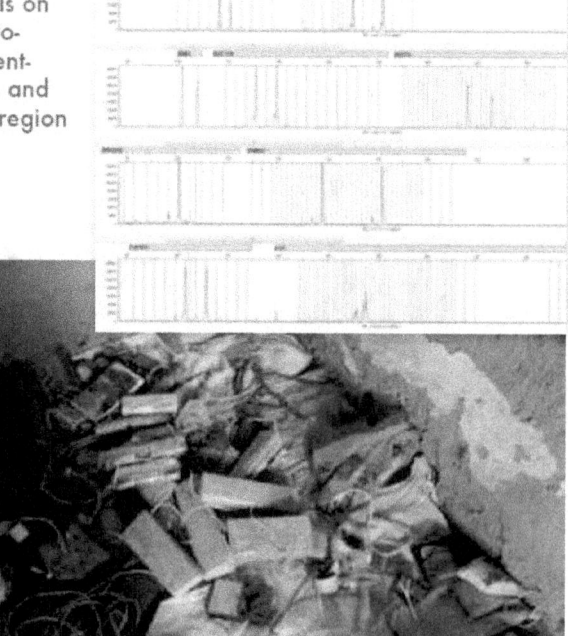

Electronic Evidence

Data Recovery from Memory Components

Completed

Although electronic equipment and instruments such as mobile computing devices, smartphones, portable GPS navigators, cameras, portable audio and video recorders, and automotive engine control and safety systems are readily destroyed during explosions and transportation crashes, the memory components often survive intact. The data within these components can provide a wealth of intelligence and evidence about the related incident. General Dynamics Information Technology developed a software tool capable of extracting, interpreting, and saving the digital data recovered from the memory components of damaged electronic devices. The tool uses a graphical user interface-based software tool that is capable of advanced data mining techniques to enable exploration of raw binary data that has been imaged directly from the original memory component. It provides visualization to assist in the identification patterns in the raw data indicative of useful information. The system runs on a PC-based platform and is fully capable of exporting the data and files to other storage media as well as fully documenting the performed processes.

Forensic Intelligence

Intelligence Interviewing and Interrogation Approaches

Current

In combating terrorism and law enforcement operations, human intelligence is critical for successful results. The key to human intelligence is effective interviewing and interrogation of subjects. Insufficient research has been accomplished to successfully validate the best and most effective interviewing and interrogation procedures. Some important aspects of interrogation, which need to be explored, are the effects of culture, social conditions, and using language interpreters during interviews. The research results will then be used to

develop better techniques for U.S. forces and law enforcement personnel to employ in future operations. Applied Research Associates is developing advanced methods for interviewing and interrogation in human intelligence collection in both law enforcement and tactical intelligence environments. The research will look to improve the understanding of effective and productive interviewing and interrogation of subjects, witnesses, and persons of interest. Additionally, it will advance the understanding of human communication, memory, social influence, and ethnic effects on interviewing and interrogation and use these findings to develop more effective interviewing procedures.

Identity Knowledge

Separation of Complex DNA Mixtures

Completed

Terrorists and criminals frequently leave DNA evidence at crime scenes or other locations that can be used to identify them and where they have been. The DNA identification techniques are now so powerful and sensitive that multiple sources of DNA often are found in a sample. This usually prevents a positive identification of any of the persons who are a source of the DNA in the mixture. If the DNA can be separated and then analyzed, these mixed samples can provide an incredible amount of evidence and intelligence value. The Bode Technology Group developed a procedure that separates samples with multiple sources of DNA by using mitochondrial DNA and Y chromosomal single tandem repeats. The process allows individual DNA profiles to be obtained from these different sources. The procedure works on samples with as many as seven different DNA sources and has a relatively rapid turnaround.

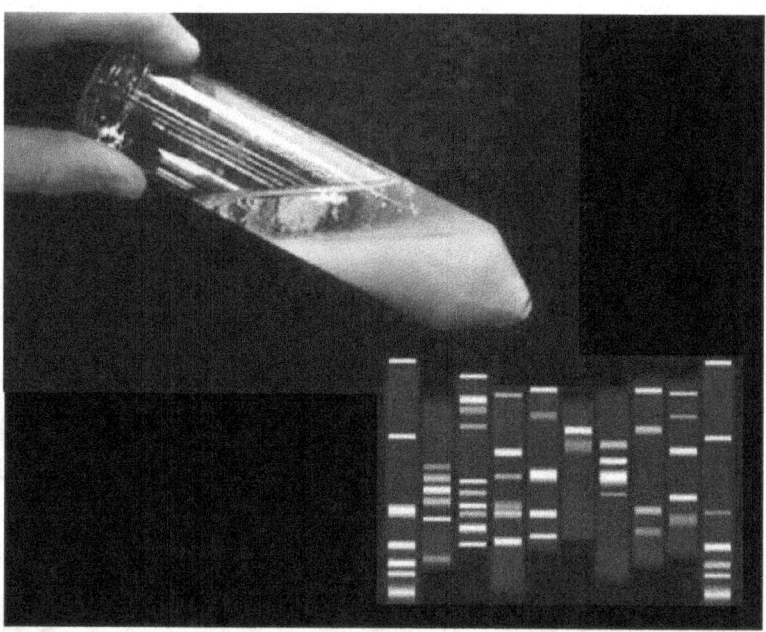

Computational analysis methods included in the overall process provide greater resolving power. The project also ensured that the procedures met the Daubert legal standards to make the results admissible in court.

Concurrent Recovery from Fingerprints and Explosive Residues

Completed

A major problem facing U.S. troops is the wide range of improvised explosive devices being employed by the enemy. With minimal training and access to explosive materials, terrorist groups or individuals can easily manufacture a variety of deadly IEDs to be used in combat. In the process of handling these IEDs, it is highly probable that fingerprints will be left at bomb sites or weapon caches with explosive residues intermixed in them. The isolation and identification of these residues can be an extremely valuable piece of intelligence. In an international effort with the Australian government and the University of Canberra, a routine fingerprint detection method was developed that concurrently recovers and analyzes explosive residues in a fingerprint. The project determined to what extent routine fingerprint methods may affect subsequent recovery and analysis of explosive residues as well as what substrates are more likely to retain explosive residues after fingerprint processing has been completed. By the end of the undertaking, guidelines were generated to show how items should be processed for latent fingerprint evidence when subsequent explosive residue analysis is possible.

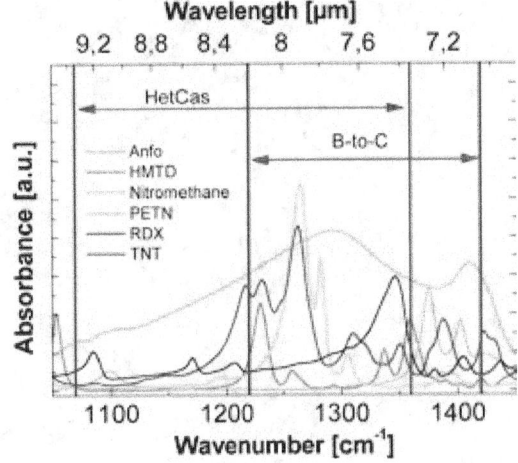

PERSONNEL PROTECTION

Mission

Identify, prioritize, and execute research and development projects that satisfy interagency requirements to provide advanced tools, techniques, and guidelines that enhance personal security.

The Personnel Protection Subgroup develops new equipment, reference tools, and standards to improve the protection of high-risk personnel (HRP). Projects focus on putting innovative tools such as automated information management systems, communication devices, mobile surveillance systems, as well as personnel and vehicle protection equipment in the hands of those tasked with the safety of HRP. The subgroup delivers new technologies to military, federal, state, and local law enforcement protection details.

ppsubgroup@cttso.gov

Focus Areas

Communications, Surveillance, and Reconnaissance

Develop technologies that provide military and law enforcement personnel with a greater capability of covertly communicating and collecting surveillance data to identify and mitigate terrorist threats against personnel. Develop technology that enhances situational awareness of mission operations.

Individual Protection and Survivability

Enhance the protection of personnel during blast and ballistic events. Develop technologies that increase the performance of body armor by reducing weight and optimizing material performance. Develop test devices and procedures that provide more biofidelic responses during blast and ballistic testing events in order to mitigate the probability of personnel injury. Quantify the effects of conventional and enhanced blast damage mechanisms to the body.

Information Resources

Develop reference materials, information management, and analytical tools to improve mission preparation, facilitate decision making, and advance incident response capabilities. Enhance software tools to more efficiently exploit intelligence and surveillance data. Generate tools that will augment the detection of networks, relationship resolution, and tracking terrorists through large amounts of data.

Mobile Security

Enhance personnel security protection during vehicular, marine, and air transportation. Develop techniques to increase protection against blast and ballistic threats during transit. Conduct performance evaluations and studies to assess the protection capabilities of transport mechanisms, and generate solutions to optimize protection.

Communications, Surveillance, and Reconnaissance

Instant Eye

Completed

Today's warfighter is often operating in small units far from support elements, including unmanned aerial system (UAS) assets. A stealthy overhead intelligence, surveillance, and reconnaissance (ISR) asset can be launched from behind cover to gain situational awareness, allowing the soldiers to effectively and safely conduct their missions. Physical Sciences, Inc. (PSI) developed Instant Eye, a small unmanned aerial system that provides the individual solider with instantaneous overhead video surveillance. The Instant Eye is launched by a soldier and directed to position where its onboard video cameras can view the targeted area. It can operate effectively in stressing combat environments, with autonomous features that enable the UAS to hold position until repositioned, recalled, or discarded. The Mk-3 Instant Eye was delivered in August 2013, with improved flight duration, wind performance, and durability over the Mk-2. The UAS weighs less than one pound and features a forward, 45 degrees, and downward looking electro-optical cameras, an IR illuminator payload for night operations, digital communication with a range of 1,000 m line-of-sight, and ruggedized propellers that are impervious to grass and minor crashes. The Mk-3 can sustain winds up to 30 mph and has a maximum speed of 35 mph and a 30-minute battery life. Video is captured on the ground control station's micro SD card, enabling soldiers to include photographs and stored video in their reporting packages. The UAS is field-repairable and low cost at less than $1,000, making it an expendable item. Up to four Instant Eye systems can operate within the same mission space. PSI developed a basic operator course in conjunction with the U.S. Army Special Operations Aviation Command and U.S. Army Special Forces Command (USAFC(A)), and the program of instruction was approved by the U.S. Army Aviation Center of Excellence Directorate of Training and Doctrine. The first course was held in September 2013, and 15 students were certified to pilot the Instant Eye. The trained pilots will deploy with the 27 kits, delivered in September 2013, to multiple combat areas during the first quarter of fiscal year 14. USAFC(A) has coordinated with Program Executive Office for Special Reconnaissance, Surveillance, and Exploitation at United States Special Operations Command to transition Instant Eye to a program of record.

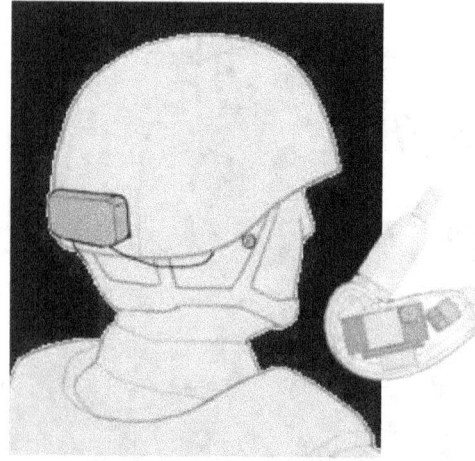

Multi-Functional Earpiece

Current

Hearing injuries decrease troop readiness and negatively impact soldier performance during service as well as lead to a reduced future quality of life. Improved hearing protection will increase soldier readiness and provide for enhanced quality of life in the years following service. The earpiece needs to address three important needs faced by today's armed forces such as hearing protection, hearing amplification, and acceleration monitoring due to blast or blunt exposure. In addressing this requirement, Sound Innovations is developing the Multi-Functional Earpiece (MFE). The MFE will provide a more comfortable in-ear hearing protection, amplification that improves the soldier's battlefield performance by enhancing his hearing and resulting situational awareness, suppression of loud noises due to blast, and will measure/record head accelerations during blast and blunt impacts. Noises between 0 and 30 decibels shall be increased by 20 decibels for hearing amplification. This system will be compatible with the Army Advanced Combat Helmet and all other equipment worn by the soldier. The earpiece will only be active when recording acceleration. Active and passive noise cancellation will provide pulse and steady rate noise protection.

Individual Protection and Survivability

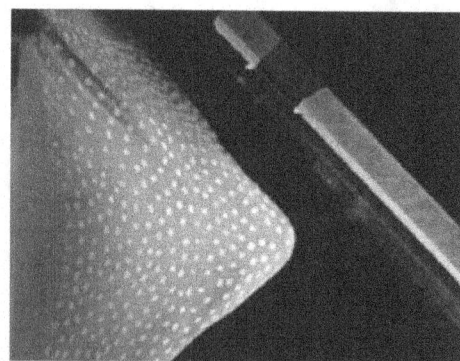

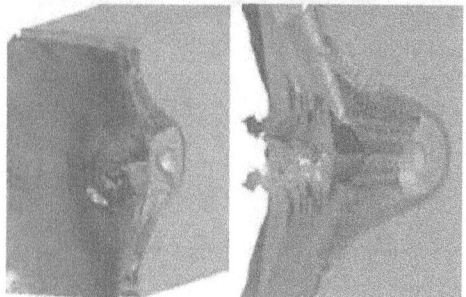

Behind Armor Blunt Trauma Mitigation

Completed

Law enforcement and military personnel wearing soft body armor suffer mild to extreme and potentially fatal internal injuries as a result of behind armor blunt trauma (BABT) of a non-penetrating ballistic round. The frequency and severity of such injuries can be reduced by a soft armor that significantly reduces the effects of BABT through a decreased backface signature (BFS). The Southwest Research Institute conducted modeling and simulation to design and assess the backface signature of candidate fabric armors. Following verification testing, two final designs underwent validation testing based on NIJ standards. Verification test results indicate a 15 percent BFS reduction for a weight neutral design and a 21 percent BFS reduction with a 10 percent weight increase, based on comparison with a standard soft armor package (28 plies of 600 denier, KM2 style 706 fabric in a 36x36 plain weave configuration). Additional designs based on carbon nanotube (CNT) materials showed great potential for reducing BFS; however, the current cost of CNT materials make those designs cost prohibitive. Test results were provided to the National Institute of Science and Technology for consideration when updating BFS limits for body armor.

Low Level Repeated Blast

Current

Substantial evidence suggests that multiple, sub-clinical, blows to the head can cause cumulative, permanent damage to the brain. It is also known that if the blows are within a certain time interval, they have a much more serious effect than if they are spaced far enough apart that the brain can recover. As a result of this data collection, Defense Advanced Research Projects Agency (DARPA) and the Department of Defense have developed blast energy sensors that can be worn on individual soldiers to record the amplitude and duration of blast waves. In addition to better understanding the injury mechanism, Applied Research Associates is currently researching the injury thresholds for clinically significant changes in neurological function caused by repeated blast exposure to low-level explosions. They will then explore the hypothesis that cumulative neurological injury occurs after repeated blast exposure and that there is an identifiable threshold where injury is significantly more likely to occur based on the cumulative pressure impulse exposure over a given time period. The goal is that once the research has been completed, the soldiers will be provided with blast exposure threshold charts. These charts will provide those who are frequently exposed to blast events with the ability to estimate their risk of injury and determine when to seek medical attention as they remove themselves from potential and additional exposures to reduce the probability of brain injury.

Information Resources

Massive Projectile Whole Body Displacement

Current

During large blast attacks on vehicles, ships, buildings, and structures, a significant source of personnel injuries is blunt trauma caused by massive projectile impacts or acceleration of unsecured individuals into rigid bodies such as walls, ceilings, floors, or equipment. The need exists to quantitatively characterize the nature and severity of these types of injuries in sufficient detail to quantify weapon effects, predict incapacitation, and anticipate medical response requirements and outcomes. To address this need, Applied Research Associates (ARA) is currently validating the sufficiency of existing injury criteria and developing new criteria to address whole body blunt impact injury mechanisms. ARA is developing a model to quantitatively characterize the nature and severity of injuries caused by 15 to 1,000 pound projectiles impacting personnel at velocities less than 200 miles per hour, incorporating both the acceleration and deceleration aspects of whole body displacement. Data analysis will yield not only injury thresholds, but also full risk of injury functions as well. The resulting model will be suitable for use in an engineering code (as opposed to a first principles model like LS-DYNA) and be capable of operating as a standalone model as well.

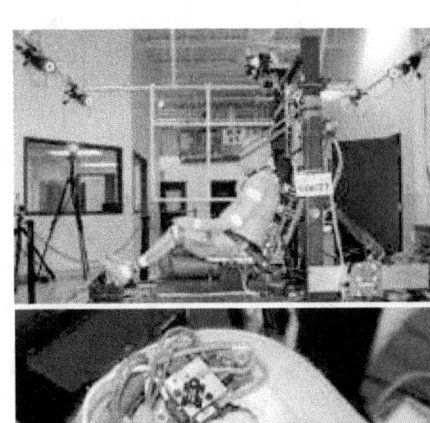

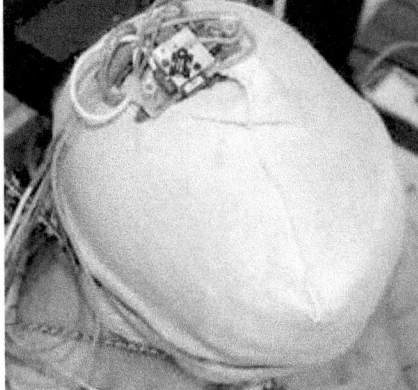

Mobile Security

Vehicle in Crowd

Completed

Armored personnel or military vehicles must have the ability to quickly maneuver through crowds of unarmed but non-compliant and/or aggressive people in a way that protects both the occupants of the vehicle and the people within the crowd. Traditional methods of crowd control that make use of less-than-lethal munitions are sometimes deemed unacceptable because of the offensive perception that comes with their use. Applied Research Associates, Inc. has developed the Integrated Conveyance Escort (ICE) system. The ICE system employs small sound generators, placed inconspicuously on the host vehicle, to deliver a variable acoustic output at frequencies below the audible range, maintaining a 10-meter standoff. The ICE system also includes a high frequency, modulated electrical pulse that may be used in the case of individuals persistent on making contact with the vehicle despite the discomfort of the sound generators. The operators within the vehicle can choose to regulate delivered electrical pulses as well as couple them with the acoustic signals to selected zones. The ICE system is operated independently of the vehicle's power, with permanent vehicle modifications, and fits within a single 6,000 cubic inch transit case.

PHYSICAL SECURITY

Mission

Identify and prioritize interagency physical security requirements to protect forces, vital equipment, and facilities against terrorist attacks; execute research and development projects that address those requirements; and transition successful prototypes into programs of record or into immediate field use to meet urgent operational needs.

pssubgroup@cttso.gov

Focus Areas

Blast Effects and Mitigation

Develop projects to satisfy interagency and international requirements that address blast threats and blast mitigation efforts to protect expeditionary and permanent structures. Emphasis will be on developing decision support tools and field raids; testing to evaluate infrastructure blast response to advance technologies to harden infrastructure; and to improve design standards, retrofits, and new threat mitigation criteria.

Emerging Explosive Threats

Develop projects to satisfy interagency and international requirements that address the adaptive threat associated with emerging explosives. Emphasize characterization of explosives and novel delivery techniques to combat their use in terrorist activities. Coordinate requirements received from the Homemade Explosives Working Group across appropriate CTTSO programs.

Vulnerability Identification

Develop predictive analysis software and decision aids to identify vulnerabilities and/ or determine preventative courses of action. Emphasize pre-event planning and assessment of emerging threats.

Screening, Surveillance, and Detection

Develop technologies and techniques to survey and analyze facilities; improve situational awareness; detect, identify, and locate advancing threats; control access to critical assets; and neutralize confirmed threats. Emphasize automatic alerting, expeditionary kits, and exportable variants.

Integrated Solutions

Integrate technologies into force protection solution packages that will improve the effectiveness of electronic security systems, reduce manning requirements, and offer increased affordability and survivability of operators and responders.

Working Groups

The Physical Security Subgroup hosts regularly scheduled working group meetings that bring together scientists, researchers, intelligence officers, operators, and academia from the interagency and international communities to collaborate on efforts, identify capability gaps, and build a collective path forward. The following five areas have active working groups: Subterranean Operations, Homemade Explosives, Vehicle Barriers, Video Analytics, and Waterside Security.

Blast Effects and Mitigation

Enhanced Forced Entry Ballistic, Blast Resistant Door

Current

To better protect U.S. embassies and facilities from hostile attacks and allow egress after a forced entry, ballistic, or blast event, the Enhanced Forced Entry Ballistic, Blast Resistant (FEBR) Door will maintain its integrity while closed during an event and is designed to remain operational to allow egress after the event. The Enhanced FEBR Door will have Americans with Disabilities Act code-sized openings and satisfy fire safety egress methods. The door will be normal in appearance and dimensionally consistent with traditional hollow metal doors. Furthermore, it will meet industry and government standards applicable to hollow metal and security doors, to include the Department of State's Certification Standard for Forced Entry Ballistic Resistance of Structural Systems.

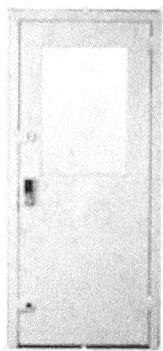

Emerging Explosive Threats

HME Desensitization Guidebook

Completed

Homemade explosives (HME) desensitization methods are being taught without scientific safety data. As a result, operators are using methods of desensitization that have not been validated. Rocky Mountain Scientific Laboratories was tasked with developing a technical reference that describes the effectiveness of current agents in the field and procedures for the desensitization of various homemade explosive mixtures and compounds. A comprehensive and systematic approach was developed to safely evaluated desensitization methods based on type of agent, sample size, and environmental effects. The results are compiled into a user-friendly technical reference and formatted in two versions: a desk reference and a Web/mobile-compatible version. The technical reference includes high resolution photographs, detailed procedures, and appropriate precautions and warnings to accurately convey the desensitization methodologies. It should be noted that the proposed methods for HME desensitization are based on current concepts of operations and are not to be regarded as best practice. The information provided in the technical reference is not meant to be an endorsement of technique, but rather, it is meant to supply safety information on practices that have been previously used in operations. The approach to testing is to identify the minimum desensitization agent ratio that would desensitize the HME when subjected to

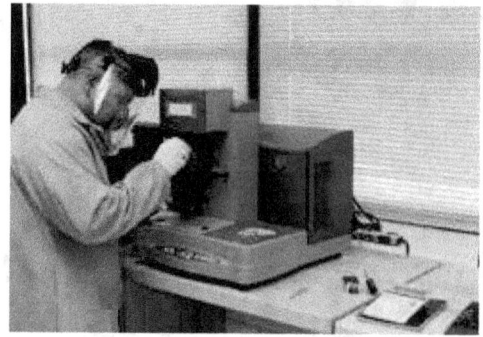

various insults. The HMEs evaluated are grouped in different categories such as fertilizer-based explosives, black powder, erythritol tetranitrate, peroxide-based explosives, potassium chlorate- based explosives, and other commonly used HMEs. Desensitization agents include a variety of products normally carried on a dismounted operation.

Screening, Surveillance, and Detection

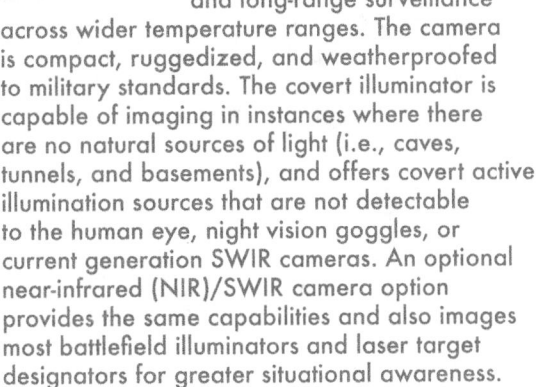

Next Generation SWIR Camera

Completed

The Next Generation Short Wave Infrared (SWIR) Camera, with its illuminator, is designed to aid operators with visual identification of potential threats in low/no light conditions. This effort has built upon past developments to produce a smaller, more easily deployable field system for use in both law enforcement and military operations. The Next Generation SWIR system is designed for both day and night surveillance and includes an illuminator and three lenses to support short, medium, and long-range surveillance across wider temperature ranges. The camera is compact, ruggedized, and weatherproofed to military standards. The covert illuminator is capable of imaging in instances where there are no natural sources of light (i.e., caves, tunnels, and basements), and offers covert active illumination sources that are not detectable to the human eye, night vision goggles, or current generation SWIR cameras. An optional near-infrared (NIR)/SWIR camera option provides the same capabilities and also images most battlefield illuminators and laser target designators for greater situational awareness.

Coral SD Upgrade to SD-2

Completed

Development and fielding of anomaly detection systems using new techniques of distinguishing objects is important to maintaining protection against explosive and weapon threats. The upgrade of the Coral SD to the Coral SD-2 system provides an improved capability for detection of explosive and weapon threats in operational environments. The system detects surface anomalies located on personnel and also in brick, drywall, and wooden walls. The Coral SD-2 is ideal for anti-terrorist operations, entry control points, controlled access facility security, and crowd screening. Upgraded improvements include a first of its kind auto-focus, additional algorithms to detect anomalies in black and white mode, and an enhanced image to increase the probability of detection for concealed person-borne threats. The Coral SD-2 can be employed as a handheld or vehicle-mounted device or through a remote operating station.

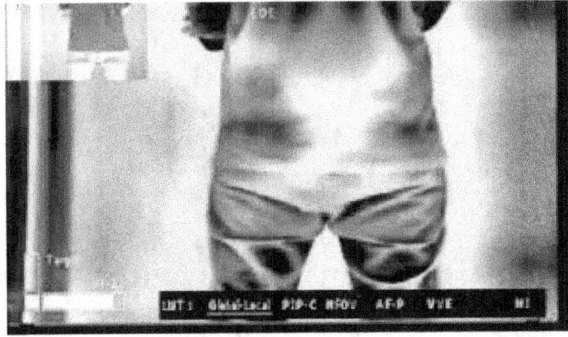

Integrated Solutions

Modular Air Droppable Force Protection Kit

Current

Currently, military forces lack a force protection system that can be packaged into one container and air dropped into austere locations. The Modular Air Droppable Force Protection Kit (MADFPK) , weighing in at just 150 pounds, will be the first air droppable expeditionary force protection kit that small units can operate in remote terrain, independent of infrastructure support. The MADFPK can be operated by one person using the control station, which displays the feeds from multiple mini-radar component systems providing 360-degree situational awareness for small compound perimeter security as well as for operations outside the compound. The kit can be used either wirelessly or as a wired system using CAT 5 cables. It will detect personnel out to 1 kilometer and vehicles out to 1.5 kilometers while providing perimeter intrusion alerts out to 500 meters. The modular system integrates a number of capabilities, including mini-radar, wire-break alerts, and camera systems with electro-optic/infrared capabilities. It contains a power-over-Ethernet adaptor, Ethernet and serial plugs, a charger port, and WiFi capability, and can operate for 12 hours on a single charge. The MADFPK system will also record alerts/events and have multi-speed video playback.

SURVEILLANCE, COLLECTION, AND OPERATIONS SUPPORT

Mission

Identify, prioritize, and execute research and development projects that satisfy interagency requirements supporting intelligence collection and special operations directed against terrorist activities.

The Surveillance, Collection, and Operations Support (SCOS) Subgroup identifies high-priority requirements and special technology initiatives focused primarily on countering terrorism through offensive operations. SCOS research and development projects enhance U.S. capabilities to conduct retaliatory or preemptive operations and to reduce the capabilities and support available to terrorists.

scossubgroup@cttso.gov

Focus Areas

Biometrics, Recognition, Identity Management, Tracking, and Exploitation (BRITE)

Improve the means to detect terrorists by developing automated tools for terrorist identification using biometrics, pattern recognition, database technologies, and exploitation methodologies.

Technical Surveillance

Develop and improve the ability to locate, identify, and track terrorists and terrorist activities. Support programs and initiatives critical to intelligence operations such as tagging, tracking, and locating; special sensors; and covert communications.

Canine Advanced Technologies

Develop methodologies that enable working canine teams to operate more effectively and efficiently by enhancing canines' abilities for explosives detection, tracking, patrolling, and offensive capabilities in an operational environment.

Counter-Surveillance Support

Develop advanced automated tools to defeat adversarial surveillance methodologies. Develop technologies to assist tactical teams with verification of assets and more effective use of interrogation data.

Human Language Technology

Develop and insert human language technologies where these technologies can best assist humans – operators and analysts – to: make sense of volumes and varieties of data sources; apply timely and actionable intelligence; enhance communication skills and cultural understanding; and improve language learning.

Photo by U.S. Army Sgt. William Begley, RC-East PAO

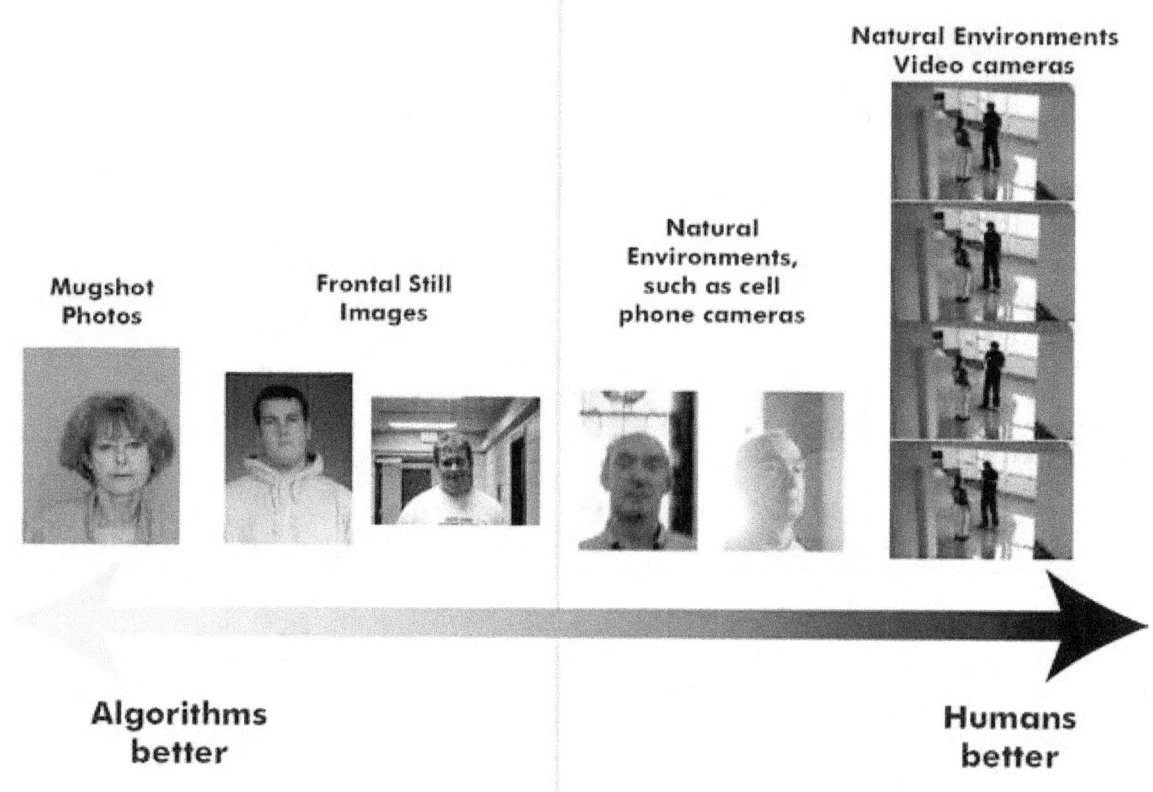

Biometrics, Recognition, Identity Management, Tracking, and Exploitation (BRITE)

ALICE

Current

Biometrics recognition algorithms have been developed intensively over the past years and have been evaluated comparatively. Concurrently during that period, human versus machine performance has been integrated into biometric challenge problems and evaluations. These performance evaluations provide valuable benchmarks for the performance of algorithms. Results have shown that machines have an advantage over humans in frontal face stills, but also have a significant disadvantage to human performance on images and video taken in natural—or uncontrolled—environments. The human visual system is still providing the benchmarks needed for the challenging tasks of developing algorithms to operate in natural operational environments. This effort assesses biometric recognition of performance of humans versus machines with datasets used in government challenges and evaluations.

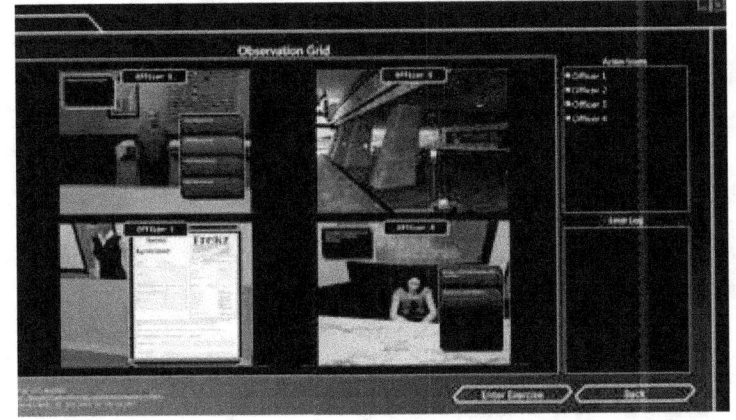

Yukon 2.0

Current

The intelligence community, military, and law enforcement have been exploring different methods and techniques to help make learning and training for a specific mission engaging and interactive for several years. Current "hands on" training methods used to meet this goal is limited in availability, is off-site (geographically), has high overhead and support structure, and is not generally conducive to current operations. This is unfortunate, as the necessity for training must grow to meet the increasing need for well-trained counterterrorism experts. The purpose of this project is to develop and enhance state-of-the-art training leveraging immersive, interactive simulation technology.

Human Language Technology

Advanced Translation Tools

Current

The rating of human translation tests is an expensive, time consuming, laborious, and critical task that the government requires when hiring professional translators. The project's goal is to computerize the test administration process, increase the speed and consistency of ratings, and improve testing analytics while reducing costs. This is made possible by applying two novel concepts: (i) millions of correct translations of each test sentence are first constructed using a specialized tool – Hybrid Translation Edit Rating (HyTER™), whose development was originally sponsored by DARPA; (ii) statistical prediction software is subsequently used to automatically rate test sentences produced by translators. Initial experiments have shown that the software can reliably predict the ratings of translators produced in three key languages – Chinese, Russian, and Spanish – in a matter of minutes with the automated tool versus manual test rating, which could take weeks or months.

This effort will add new languages, including Arabic, Farsi, and Hebrew, and will deploy an operational capability at the FBI.

Culturally Authentic Materials Management between Institutions

Current

The Culturally Authentic Materials Management between Institutions (CAMMI) project is the hub for hosting culturally authentic multimedia multilingual materials from various sources (broadcast video, Web text, images, and social media content) and providing accounts to various Department of Defense, intelligence community, and academic language institutions. The digital objects provide users with the ability to search the content, manipulate the media, edit clips, author activities, create analytical products, and determine the dissemination permissions across institutions on multiple platforms and mobile devices. These materials will enhance cultural understanding, media analysis, and language learning.

TACTICAL OPERATIONS SUPPORT

Mission

Identify, prioritize, and execute research and development projects that enhance the capabilities of DoD and interagency special operations tactical teams engaged in finding, fixing, and finishing terrorists. This includes the development of capabilities for state and local law enforcement agencies to combat domestic terrorism.

The Tactical Operations Support (TOS) Subgroup provides technology solutions to assist surgical strike and special warfare operational personnel in a variety of tactical missions and environments. Most often these solutions are in the form of rapidly prototyped specialized equipment and training. Each capability is specifically designed to provide enhanced mission effectiveness while assisting operational personnel in maintaining situational awareness and survivability.

tossubgroup@cttso.gov

Focus Areas

Communications Systems

Develop flexible and enhanced communications capabilities specifically designed for tactical forces. Emphasize reducing operational load while improving operator mobility and efficiency. Performance factors include durability, concealment, power management, range, reception, battery life, ease of use, and low probability of exploitation. Develop assured tactical communications connectivity in challenging environments such as buildings, caves, tunnels, below deck, or underground bunkers.

Intelligence, Surveillance, Target Acquisition, and Reconnaissance Systems

Develop technologies to assist tactical teams in conducting intelligence, surveillance, target acquisition, and reconnaissance missions. Develop systems that enhance the visual perception or other imaging capabilities of tactical operators in all conditions and environments. Develop independent, vehicular, or weapon-mounted systems for enhanced aiming, target designation, illumination, range detection, or surveillance.

Offensive Systems

Develop equipment and capabilities that enhance the effectiveness of small units of dominance engaged in surgical strike operations. Develop specialized weapons, munitions, detonators, distraction/diversion devices, and other unique tactical equipment. Develop systems to support sniper and counter-sniper operations.

Survivability Systems

Develop clothing, individual equipment, mobility platform enhancements, and man-portable systems that provide protection from or identification of ballistic, fragmentation, explosive, and thermal threats during the conduct of special operations. Develop man-portable sensor systems to enhance operator security during tactical missions.

Unconventional Warfare, Counter-Insurgency Support

Develop innovative solutions for small tactical teams conducting a broad spectrum of military, paramilitary, and special warfare operations. This includes counterinsurgency and foreign internal defense missions with, by, or through host nation or indigenous forces, to build partner capacity in support of U.S. goals and objectives.

Communications Systems

Next Generation Tactical Mesh Network

Current

The Next Generation Tactical Mesh Network (NG-TacMN) is a communications relay that increases the range of communications for tactical operators and allows information to be transmitted and received with increased fidelity and resolution. NG-TacMN incorporates both hardware and software solutions, radios, operational control units, situational awareness software, and tactical sensors. This sophisticated communications kit is capable of secure dissemination and viewing of multiple full motion video streams, point-to-point and group chat,

Voice Over IP, Blue Force Tracking, map telestration, and file transfer. NG-TacMN proof-of-concept kits and new equipment training has been delivered to several special operations tactical units for initial assessment. Operational feedback is being collected from operators to improve the software package to ensure it effectively meets operators' needs. Units will receive final production kits to conduct operational evaluations and real world domestic operations in fiscal year 14.

Intelligence, Surveillance, Target Acquisition, and Reconnaissance Systems

Micro Tactical Ground Robot

Current

Special Operations Forces (SOF) and Explosive Ordnance Disposal (EOD) units have a critical need for highly mobile, lightweight, ground robotic systems to detect, disable, and defeat the improvised explosive device threat on today's battlefield. The Micro Tactical Ground Robot (MTGR) is a tactical visual and acoustic intelligence, surveillance, and reconnaissance (ISR) robot featuring 360-degree day/night coverage from five cameras, two eye-safe laser pointers, and

an internal microphone. The MTGR is highly maneuverable in all terrains and environments with the unique ability to climb stairs and steep inclines. The MTGR remains light enough to be transported by a dismounted operator across rugged terrain over long distances, providing support to SOF and EOD conducting intelligence, surveillance, reconnaissance, and counter improvised explosive device missions. The MTGR uses a mobile mesh radio, which greatly improves the safe standoff distance for operators and noncombatants when rendering safe or emplacing an IED counter charge using its unique manipulator arm assembly. Additionally, the MTGR has an internal GPS receiver and digital magnetic compass for position reporting to ensure command and control for situational awareness and recovery.

All of these features are supported and managed by an intuitive graphical user interface (GUI) and ruggedized operator control unit to allow for decreased training time and/or need for operator specialization. The MTGR is the lightweight ground robotic system that is currently filling the tactical level combat capability gap for SOF and EOD. Units will receive final production kits to conduct operational evaluations and real world domestic operations in fiscal year 14 through fiscal year 15.

Handheld Intelligence Surveillance Target Acquisition Reconnaissance System

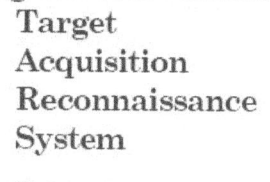

Current

The Handheld Intelligence Surveillance Target Acquisition and Reconnaissance System (HISTARS) is a multipurpose lightweight, modular system that provides Special Operations Forces with the ability to conduct enhanced terminal guidance operations and ISR. The system consists of a joint terminal attack controller laser target designator and special operations sensor for targeting and ranging. HISTARS enables the operator to identify targets at greater ranges with higher resolution optics for night operations and decreases power consumption, reducing the need to carry additional batteries, thus significantly decreasing operational load. SOF units will receive final production kits to conduct operational evaluations in fiscal year 14.

Clip-on Night Vision Device – Sensor Fusion

Current

The Clip-on Night Vision Device – Sensor Fusion (CNVD-SF) combines and enhances the capabilities of currently fielded image intensification (I2) and thermal, long-wave infrared clip-on night vision devices (CNVD and CNVD-T). The CNVD-SF eliminates the need for an operator to carry two separate clip-on night vision devices for I^2 and thermal. By utilizing a high refresh rate sensor, the CNVD-SF is able to minimize image lag between the I^2 and thermal imaging to provide operators with faster and higher performing optical enhancement during night combat operations. The CNVD-SF also features a video-out capability. CNVD-SF provides the operator with one device that does the job of two. SOF units will receive final production kits to conduct combat operational evaluations in fiscal year 14.

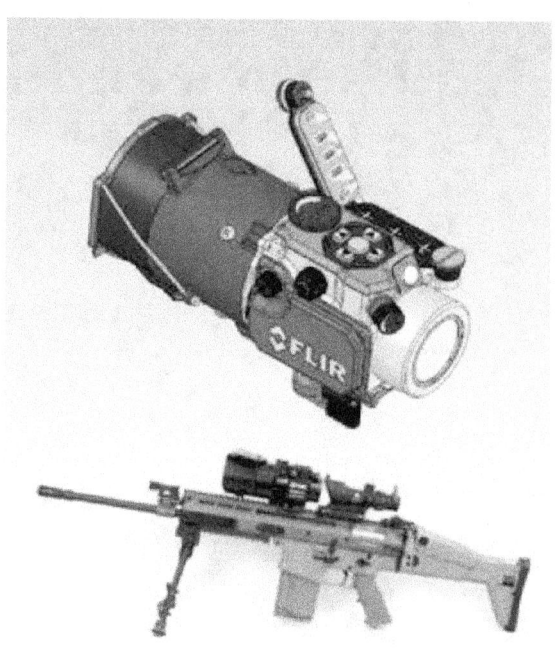

ArrowLite Small Unmanned Aerial System – Hand-Launched

Current

ArrowLite-Hand-Launched provides SOF with a state-of-the-art, leap-ahead organic aerial ISR capability that can be assembled and hand-launched in fewer than 90 seconds after removal from a waterproof transport carry case and is capable of operating for more than two and a half hours (launch to landing). The system comes with the Procerus two-axis mechanical gimbaled stabilized sensor, with laser illuminator, and operates using the mobile ad hoc (MANET) mesh network using a multi-functional ground control station (GCS) ruggedized operator control unit (ROCU) for level III flight control with full autopilot authority and additional ROCU terminals that serve as remote video terminals. The total weight of the system – to include air vehicle with payload, carrying case, MANET radios, ROCU-7 GCS, and remote viewing terminal, directional antenna with tripod, cables, and military standard batteries – is less than 13 pounds. Proof-of-concept flights, kits, and new equipment training will be delivered to several special operations tactical units for initial assessment. Operational feedback will be collected from operators to improve the software package to ensure that it effectively meets operators' needs. Units will receive final production kits to conduct operational evaluations and real world domestic operations in fiscal year 14.

Advanced Inline Thermal Sniper Sight

Current

SOF and law enforcement tactical sniper units tasked with combating terrorism require the most effective optics for precision long-range target interdiction in low light conditions. The Advanced Inline Thermal Sniper Sight (AITSS) was developed to enable effective target acquisition, identification, and engagement during low light operations to the maximum effective range of current sniper systems. The AITSS consists of a state-of-the-art uncooled thermal sensor, an electro-optical camera with electronic zoom, and a high resolution organic light emitting device display. The AITSS delivers real-time target image processing, allowing handoff from spotter to sniper through a visible laser marker in the thermal video display. The AITSS assists rapid spotter/sniper target handoff for precision long range, low light target engagement with "right target, right time, every time" finality. Units will receive final production kits and conduct combat operational evaluations in fiscal year 14.

Offensive Systems

Enhanced Mortar Targeting System – Mobile

Current

United States Special Operations Forces deployed to high threat locations globally require an organic, highly-accurate, rapid, and mobile indirect fire capability for force protection. The Enhanced Mortar Targeting System – Mobile (EMTAS – Mobile) incorporates a state-of-the-art enhanced ballistic computer with an 81 mm mortar integrated on a highly mobile light commercial vehicle with enhanced suspension. The entire system is provided as a kit to allow for quick installation in austere environments. With only two operators, the EMTAS-Mobile is ready to fire in less than 45 seconds, delivering lethal consequence to the enemy, 360 degrees, out to 5.5 km with a circular error probability of 1 percent. This capability enhances the speed, accuracy, and reliability of legacy weapons and ammunition. The EMTAS-Mobile provides the operator with a highly accurate, highly

mobile, and low-visibility indirect fire support platform that improves small unit and host nation personnel survivability while minimizing the risk of collateral damage. Units will receive final production kits to conduct operational evaluations in fiscal year 14 through fiscal year 15

Unconventional Warfare, Counter-Insurgency Support

Social Media Mobile Training Teams

Completed

Social media has become a primary means of communication globally. This medium is being leveraged by state and non-state actors to coordinate and conduct illegal and terrorist activities against U.S. and allied interests. At the request of SOF, CTTSO is providing social media mobile training to SOF tactical level leaders, units, and families at their home stations to disseminate information on the social media threat and landscape for force protection and mission planning. This training enables units to deploy forward with the skills, tools, and best practices to exploit open source social media information to increase situational awareness in their areas of operation. More advanced courses are being coordinated at the users' requests and will continue in fiscal year 14.

WATSON

Current

The United States continues to encounter an increasing cyber threat where a "digital divide" exists between the U.S. and its cyber opponents. The larger government and military organizations are standing up capacities and capabilities to address this threat at the strategic level. At the request of SOF, CTTSO has taken the initiative to complement this larger build by training operators at the tactical level. WATSON is an unclassified, open source digital operations course tailored to train tactical operators to understand the cyber domain and to identify and mitigate cyber threats. The four-week course provides foundations in computer science, information security, social media, social engineering, and advanced computer networking. This classroom instruction is validated in over 20 practical field training exercises. Tactical operators trained at WATSON return to their units as master trainers in cyber tactics, techniques, and procedures. The digital domain will become key terrain on future battlefields. WATSON continues in fiscal year 14 to contribute to the development of future SOF capabilities for 21st Century special warfare.

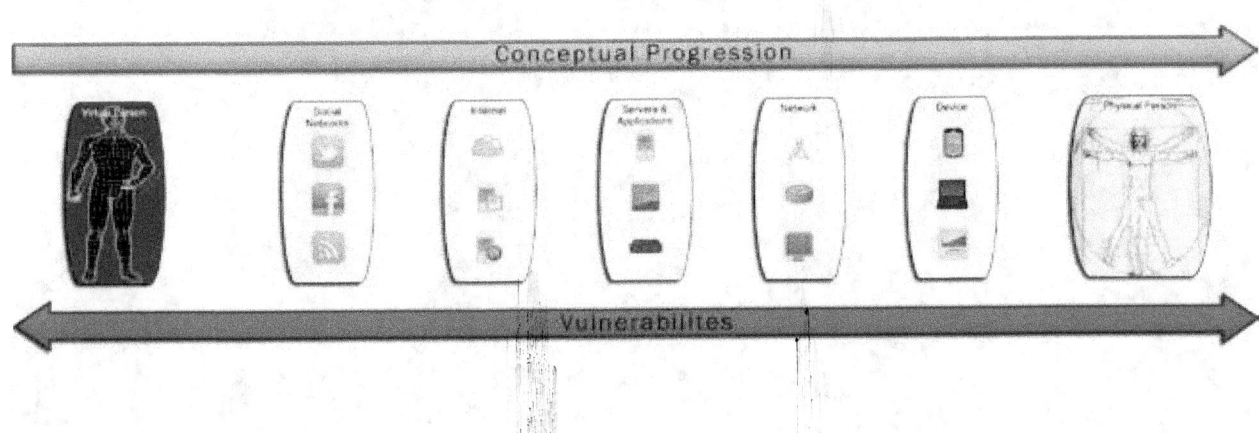

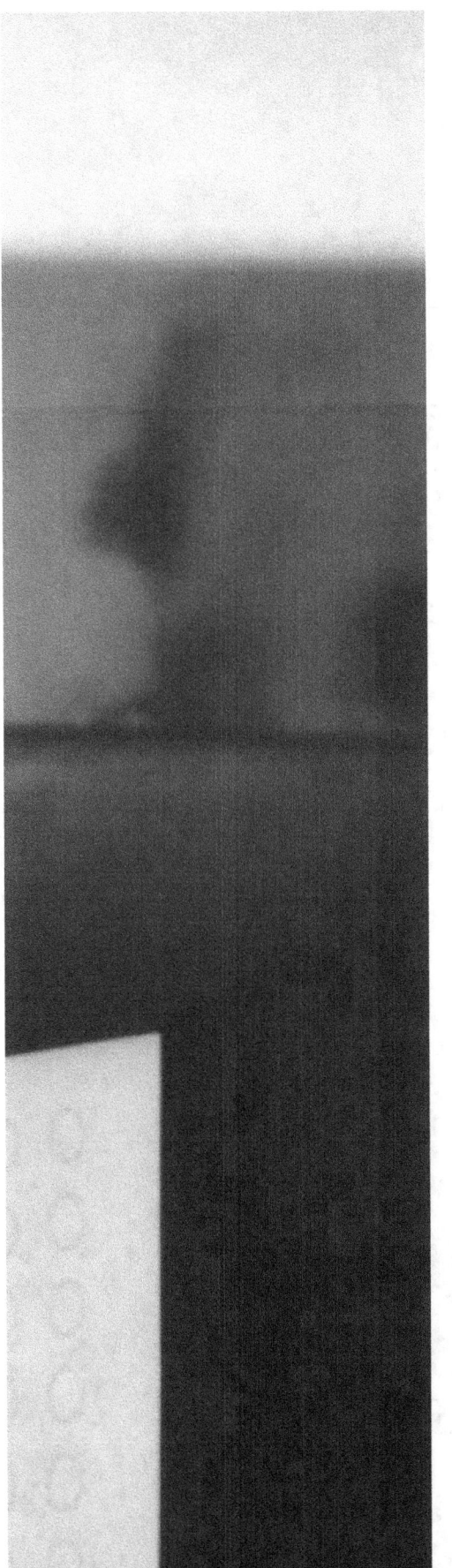

TRAINING TECHNOLOGY DEVELOPMENT

Mission

Identify, prioritize, and execute projects that satisfy interagency requirements for the development and delivery of combating terrorism related education, training, and mission performance support products and technologies.

The Training Technology Development (TTD) Subgroup delivers training and training technologies to increase mission readiness and enhance operational capabilities in the combating terrorism community. The strategy behind the mission is to analyze, design, develop, integrate, evaluate, and leverage distributed learning technologies to deliver high-quality training and education in the medium best suited to the users' needs and requirements. A representative from the United States Special Operations Command (USSOCOM) chairs the subgroup.

ttdsubgroup@cttso.gov

Focus Areas

Advanced Training and Education

Develop programs of instruction, training packages, and computer- and classroom-based terrorism training courses. Develop the advanced tools, techniques, and guidelines required to analyze needs, develop solutions, and evaluate results. Analyze performance needs to identify applicable solutions. Integrate and deliver technologies with combating terrorism training materials to increase the quality, effectiveness, and accessibility of training.

Human Performance Technology

Analyze the full range of human performance gaps and select interventions to improve and sustain human performance. Develop enabling performance improvement technologies and performance devices to enhance the performance of operators during training missions. Develop job aids, best practices, human factors interactions, selection and motivation interventions, and performance support systems.

Mobile Learning

Utilize mobile technology to deliver interactive learning solutions and applications for end users that can be accessed anytime and from anywhere. Develop mobile capabilities that support learning through ubiquitous access to performance support, educational resources, collaboration, user-generated content, and learning solutions for use in the classroom or in support of distance education.

Models, Simulations, and Games

Develop interactive models, simulations, and games (MS&G), including, but not limited to: tabletop simulations, field exercise simulations, immersive virtual-learning environments, hands-on virtual reality, simulation models, and PC-based three-dimensional and isometric simulations and games. Develop crowd models, adversarial behavior models, network-based simulations, and mini-simulations on specific combating terrorism related tasks. Incorporate beneficial game characteristics through the full range of game genres (i.e., strategy, first person tactical, massively multiplayer online game, role-playing, etc.). Develop tools, technologies, and techniques for improving MS&G design, development, and validation.

Photo by Sgt. Joseph Guenther

  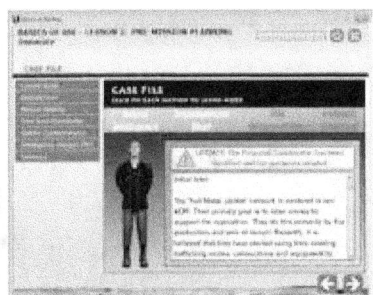

Advanced Training and Education

Sensitive Site Exploitation

Current

Sensitive site exploitation (SSE) training is specific to an AOR or a job function. The Forensic Innovation Center designed and developed a self-paced site exploitation course that is independent of an AOR and applicable to those who need to know the basics and tactical applications of SSE. Targeted at three distinct levels—basic, tactical, and ideal—the training allows students to receive the support they need to successfully exploit a site. It is appropriate for military or non-military collectors, analysts, or operators. Lessons are supported by multimedia events, interactive exercises, and simulations.

The Sensitive Site Exploitation training provides a holistic overview of SSE procedures through a widely accessible computer/Web-based training program for military and nonmilitary intelligence personnel, independent of any area of operation. The interactive training program, which consists of 10 lessons, provides insight into the entire SSE process and how an individual's respective roles and responsibilities related to mission efforts come before and after mission execution.

Human Performance Technology

Enhancing Sensory Performance

Current

To increase the operator's ability to sense, process, and react to threats, identify and engage targets, and remember and report details of actions, White Canvas Group is looking at the full performance spectrum to develop and evaluate a program designed to enhance visual sensory skill performance to move warfighters and law enforcement from normal to elite performance levels. The capability will test operators' visual and sensory performance to establish a baseline, develop a customized performance improvement plan, implement the program through visual and sensory exercises, and re-test to evaluate performance improvement and system effectiveness.

Training Technology Development

Mobile Learning

Gas Chromatographer-Mass Spectrometer

Current

Mobile applications, better known as apps, are an effective performance support tool for delivering information to users immediately prior to and/or during task performance. Training on a piece of equipment often occurs months before operational use, resulting in much of the training being forgotten by time of need. Adayana Government Group designed and developed a software solution and mobile

application to support the use of the Gas Chromatographer-Mass Spectrometer (GC-MS). GC-MS is an analytical instrument that can be used for detection, identification, and quantification of chemical warfare agents and toxic industrial chemicals. The mobile application provides an overview of the features, functions, and general procedures of the GC-MS to re-familiarize users with the system and guide them through operational tasks. This research and development effort lays the groundwork for future app development that augments training to support operational use.

Models, Simulations, and Games

Parachute Simulator

Current

Developing Special Forces (SF) skills for high altitude–low opening (HALO) or high altitude–

high opening (HAHO) operations requires a significant number of training hours. Though parachute training is ideally accomplished with live jumps, a number of the emergency procedures are too risky to be trained live.

To address this need, USSOCOM is implementing Parachute Training Simulators that augment the existing classroom, wind tunnel, and live jump curriculum. The current effort involves the installation and evaluation of the Systems Technology Inc. (STI) PARASIM® at the U.S. Army John F. Kennedy Special Warfare Center and School. This virtual reality simulator system allows SF to practice a wide range of emergency procedures in a highly realistic yet safe training environment. STI has installed six integrated parachute jump stations to train basic through advanced techniques before conducting a HALO or HAHO live jump. The system is currently being evaluated and upgraded concurrently to maximize operational benefits of the jump station and mission rehearsal.

Realistic Adaptive Interactive Learning System – Chemical Agent Response

Current

Military and civilian first responders often enter unknown environments that require split second decisions based on instrument responses and visual cues. Situational awareness and reaction speeds are critical for protecting life and minimizing property damage. Spectral Labs is developing the Realistic Adaptive Interactive Learning System – Chemical Agent Response (RAILS-CHEM), an interactive, 3-D game enabling responders to control simulated avatars in a wide variety of realistic hazardous environments such as illicit labs, stadium events, subway stations, and multistory buildings. RAILS-CHEM is a browser-based simulation for military and emergency response personnel on the topic of chemical agent response. It is a highly customizable tool for instructors to use to meet agency specific training needs. The simulation will integrate algorithms to depict chemical agent behaviors, handheld chemical detection systems' responses, and character exposure systems.

Learning modules range in duration and typically last from 5 to 10 minutes to accommodate schedule constraints of novice and experienced first responders. Learning paths can be customized by instructors for specific users or groups, depending on agency equipment configurations, availability, and user skill levels, in assessing the current situation and when to don personal protective equipment for different circumstances based on exposure systems.

Responders are challenged throughout the scenarios and during post-simulatoin quizzes on comprehension of material and proficiency in areas such as equipment functionality, instrument readings, and observed exposure symptoms. Depending upon course configuration, results are tabulated and provided to the trainee via a certificate and to the instructor via the software email notification system.

EXPLOSIVE ORDNANCE DISPOSAL/LOW-INTENSITY CONFLICT

Mission

The Explosive Ordnance Disposal/Low-Intensity Conflict (EOD/LIC) Program develops and delivers advanced capabilities for military Explosive Ordnance Disposal (EOD) operators and Special Operations Forces (SOF) to meet the challenges of the full spectrum of explosive hazards to include improvised explosive devices (IEDs), as well as to enhance force protection, as related to the conduct of the war on terrorism.

eodlic@eodlic.cttso.gov

Focus Areas

Access and Disablement

Develop tools to quickly and efficiently breach or gain access to structures, barriers, vehicles, and containers. Develop chemical, mechanical, electrical, and explosively actuated systems for the neutralization and disruption of unexploded ordnance and improvised devices. Improve technologies for rendering fuzing and firing systems inoperable.

Detection, Diagnostics, and Analysis

Develop tools to locate and verify the presence of improvised devices, unexploded ordnance, booby traps, and other threats. Develop technologies to determine the specific type, condition, and characteristics of unexploded ordnance and improvised device components, and the specific hazards associated with each. Improve methods to analyze and evaluate improvised device construction.

Protective Measures and Effects Mitigation

Advance the development of personnel protection systems for operations in enhanced hazard environments. Develop novel and improved solutions to protect personnel and property from blast, fragmentation, and ballistic hazards.

Remote Operations and Advanced Mobility

Develop capabilities to remotely approach, enter, and conduct reconnaissance operations in hazard areas and danger zones. Enhance mobility-related technologies and equipment to facilitate safely approaching, operating in, and withdrawing from hazardous environments. Develop systems and technologies to gather and store operational information for transmission to operational personnel and unit commanders. Improve technologies for the relocation of unexploded ordnance, hazardous materials, and improvised devices.

Sustainability and Operations Management

Develop tools and equipment to enhance situational awareness and operational capability during incident response or direct action operations. Develop human performance improvement tools that foster the advancement of knowledge related to unexploded ordnance, improvised devices, and enhanced hazard environments. Develop tools and training for conducting novel and advanced missions related to improvised devices and enhanced hazard environments.

U.S. Army photo by Staff Sgt. Michel Sauret

Access and Disablement

Electromagnetic Non-Lethal Small Boat Stopping

Completed

This was a U.S. and Singapore joint project to develop and demonstrate radio frequency sources to disrupt outboard engines on small craft. This effort involved the development and demonstration – during sea trials – of a non-lethal, high-power electromagnetic source to stop, or substantially slow small boats from a safe standoff distance. This capability would provide an additional layer of defense to stop unauthorized entry of small boats into sensitive or restricted waterways, determine the intent of intruding boats, or allow military or Coast Guard/law enforcement personnel to stop fleeing boats.

EOD Techniques for Insensitive Explosive Filled Munitions

Current

This effort involves the development of techniques and concept render safe tools capable of achieving high or low order (or both) disposals of a candidate insensitive high explosive (IHE) munition and demonstrate that in a joint U.S.-UK trial.

The U.S. and the UK have an insensitive munitions acquisition policy, and the majority of future munitions will have IHE fills. IHE fills in conventional munitions are rendering current EOD disposal techniques obsolete, as IHEs are less vulnerable to attack by shape charges, explosively formed penetrators, and projectiles. New EOD techniques are required to provide capability against IHEs in post conflict and logistic disposal operations.

Underwater Explosive Threat Toolkit

Current

Currently, U.S. Navy EOD divers and Mine Countermeasures forces have limited tools to address the threats presented by underwater mines and other underwater explosive hazards. This project involves the development of a suite of tools that includes appropriate type and size charge containers. These tools are hand-packed with explosives by divers for use in render safe procedures against underwater limpets, other mines, and improvised explosive devices for Navy EOD technicians and Mine Countermeasures Forces.

Remote Operations and Advanced Mobility

MK16 Mod 1 UBA IDDM
Underwater Breathing Apparatus, Improved Diver Display Mask

Completed

This project involved the development of an integrated, internal information display for the M48 dive mask, which is used with the low magnetic MK16 Mod 1 UBA. This display provides special operations and EOD divers with "hands-free," life support and equipment status information, irrespective of water turbidity.

EOD/LIC Fiscal Year 2013 Project Funding ($2.2M)

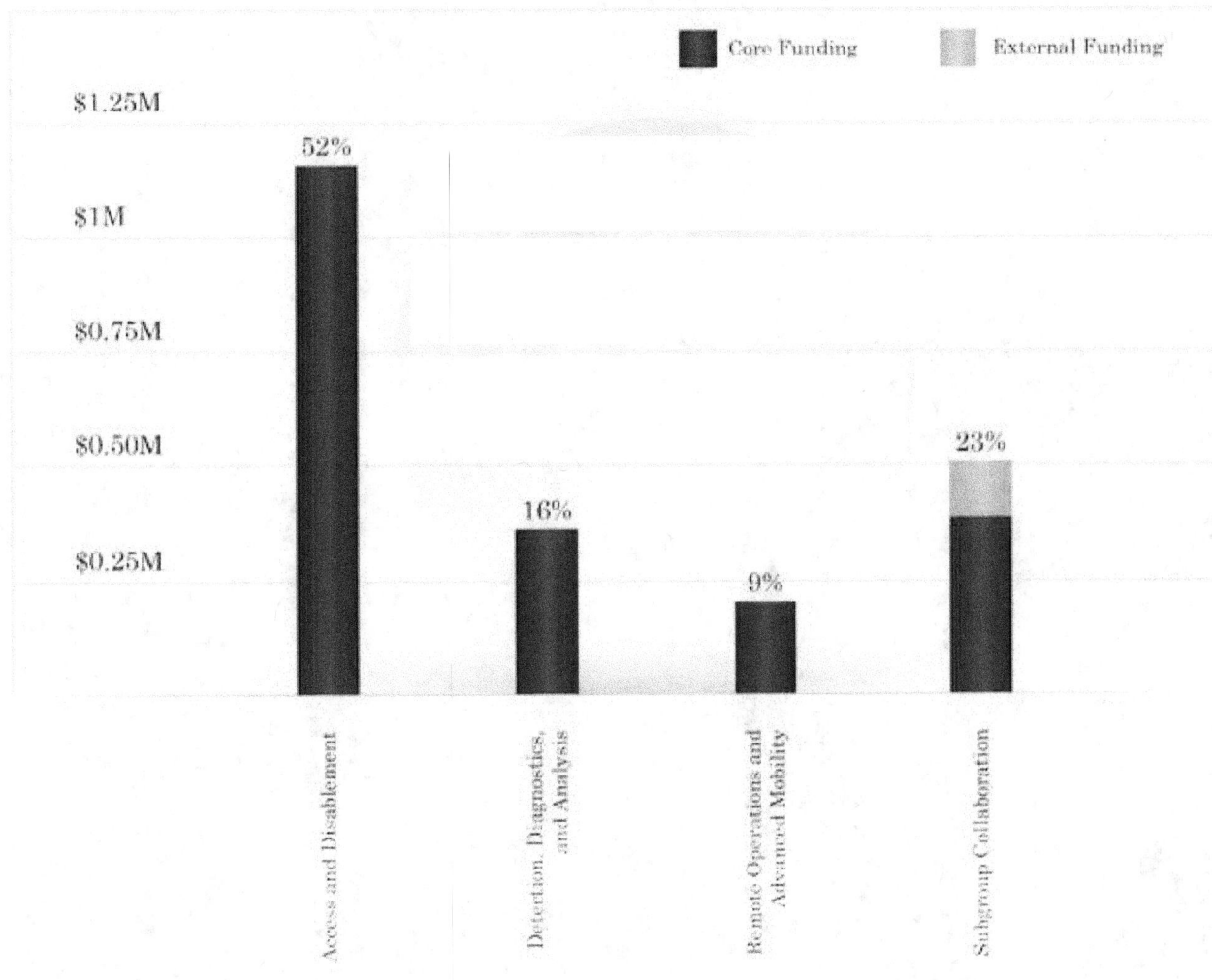

IRREGULAR WARFARE SUPPORT

Mission

Develop adaptive and agile ways and means to support irregular warfare in the current and evolving strategic environments. Support joint, interagency, and international partners who conduct irregular warfare through indirect and asymmetric approaches with solutions to erode an adversary's power, influence, and will. Identify materiel and non-materiel solutions via operational analysis, concept development, field experimentation, and spiral delivery of capabilities to defeat the motivations, sanctuaries, and enterprises of targeted state and non-state actors.

The Irregular Warfare Support Program (IWS) builds capacity and capability for irregular warfare from a defense-interagency-international perspective. It develops cross-domain blended capabilities necessary to enable sustained counterterrorism and counterinsurgency operations. This program leverages ongoing research efforts of U.S. Special Operations Command, the military departments, Defense agencies, and other federal agencies to analyze, design, prototype, and demonstrate enduring technical and operational capabilities. IWS projects blend several disciplines including tactics, operations, doctrine, policy, information, training, and technology.

iwsp@iwsp.cttso.gov

Focus Areas

Battlespace Awareness

Conduct research, operational analyses, capability design, and implementation support to enable forces to understand dispositions and intentions as well as characteristics and conditions of the threat and operational environment that influence national, coalition, interagency, and military decision making.

Building Partner Capacity

Conduct research, operational analysis, capability design, and implementation support in order to enable the Department of Defense to assist, train, advise, and influence foreign partners, foreign competitors, adversary leaders, military-like forces, and relevant populations by developing and presenting information and conducting shaping activities to affect their perceptions, will, behavior, and/or capabilities. This includes research and development that supports the conduct of communication, shaping missions, and activities, but does not include kinetic operations or maneuver of forces for the purpose of influence.

Indirect Communications Support

Conduct research, operational analysis, capability design, and implementation support within the scope of traditional military information operations to enhance and improve client organization efforts to erode adversaries' power, influence, and will through proactive and responsive informational, psychological, and other irregular operations. IWS seeks to increase the efficacy of military information operations while decreasing the likelihood of direct action.

Knowledge Management

Conduct research, operational analysis, capability design, and spiral experimentation support to increase U.S. and appropriate partners' understanding of hostile forces, current and evolving tactical and operational environments, and opportunities for successful irregular warfare operations.

Mission Rehearsal and Exercise

Conduct research, operational analysis, capability design, and implementation support to increase U.S. and coalition partners' proficiency in and capacity to wage irregular warfare on targeted state and non-state actors. IWS seeks to further the art and science of irregular warfare operations and enhanced understanding in the appropriate agencies, forces, and bodies of government.

Operations Integration

Conduct research, operational analysis, capability design, and implementation support to synchronize interagency irregular warfare efforts. IWS refines current capabilities and develops those capabilities necessary for friendly forces to prevent and prevail in future conflicts.

Pursuit and Denial

Conduct research, operational analysis, capability design, and implementation support to enable client organizations to better apply indirect and asymmetric force to identify, disrupt, deny, exploit, manipulate, and destroy hostile organizations and their supporting enterprises.

Indirect Communications Support

Social Media Exploitation to Counter Transnational Criminal Organizations

Current

The Social Media Exploitation to Counter Transnational Criminal Organizations (TCOs) project addresses a critical need for improved assessment of information operations (IO) by providing a prototype solution that helps measure changes in popular support in response to IO activities. The intent is to provide relevant, reliable feedback via a real-time data capture and analysis system capable of measuring, modeling, and forecasting changes in popular support for and influence of TCOs at the regional level. The focus for this project is the analysis of unclassified/open source and publicly available information and the respective assessment-related metadata in order to establish a baseline of TCO influence and measure changes over time. This amalgamation of information will be visualized via an information environment common operating picture allowing for data to be analyzed collectively and providing a sketch of influence and control for a specific region.

Knowledge Management

West African Sharing Portal

Current

Terrorists are increasingly employing sophisticated, network-based, transnational finance, operations, and logistical mechanisms. This makes the human-network activities of such threat entities far more difficult to detect: terrorists can exploit the "seams" between combatant commands and the interagency/law enforcement community caused by the inability to merge intelligence data, thereby impeding collaboration and making information sharing inefficient and cumbersome. To overcome these obstacles, the U.S. and its partners have, at times, been forced to work around their existing agency/organization stovepipes. These approaches are generally ineffective, frequently non-secure, and are not feasible for all Coalition or interagency partners. While some commercial "cloud-based" sharing approaches purport to solve these problems, such systems lack controllable data/user segmentation and positive control of data.

The West African Sharing Portal (WASP) is an enclave within the Irregular Warfare Support Program's Secure Unclassified Network (SUNet) project. Under SUNet, secure enclaves are developed to meet users' unique missions and use cases. SUNet key features include rapid integration of voice, data, and mission specific tools, served up in low-bandwidth environments.

The West African Sharing Portal provides a secure Internet collaboration platform for U.S. and Nigerian interagency partners with real-time information sharing access, which allows agencies to collect and consolidate data and communications resources in one secure location accessible via Web browser (i.e., on smartphones, tablet devices, and personal computers). This portal provides enhanced partner nation capability to identify, inspect, interdict, and investigate passengers involved in illicit activity.

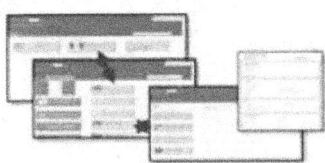

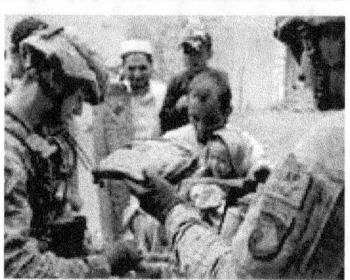

Mission Rehearsal and Exercise or Operations Integration

Insider Threat Situational Awareness Training

Completed

Irregular warfare strategies invariably require close and consistent contact with indigenous personnel. This contact is inherently risky due to inadvertent agitation of cultural norms and successful infiltration efforts by adversaries. Insider Threat Situational Awareness (IT-SAT) responds to the need for a non-materiel solution to enhance the effectiveness and survivability of advisors engaged in capacity building where the threat of insider attacks is prevalent. Risk mitigation strategies that rely upon the security screening of indigenous personnel and procedures such as physical searches in and of themselves are insufficient to protect the imbedded advisor. By instilling in the individual advisor a cognitive process for identifying and addressing potential green on blue attacks, he is armed with the capability to confront an ever-changing threat.

IT-SAT delivered a proactive methodology for recognizing threats and a decision making framework for how to take appropriate risk mitigating actions. It focused on teaching the individual advisor how to better read and interpret his environment using human behavior pattern recognition and analysis (HBPR&A). HBPR&A instills in the advisor the capability to analyze the environment using the six domains (heuristics, proxemics, geographics, kinesics, atmospherics, and biometrics) of human behavior. IT-SAT built into the advisor the ability to rapidly evaluate his environment and act prior to being acted upon, thus maintaining the initiative and mitigating insider attacks that threaten partner capacity building efforts.

IT-SAT delivered to the individual advisor an intensive three-day course delivered by a mobile training team in theater. IT-SAT has been incorporated into the U.S. Army Maneuver Center of Excellence 22-day Advanced Situational Awareness Training curriculum. Interested parties may procure IT-SAT training through the General Service Administration schedule.

Pursuit and Denial

Digital Threats and Countermeasures

Current

The Digital Threats and Countermeasures program is an effort to collect data, assess, evaluate, analyze, and determine suitability of an array of technologies and resources in support of cyber overwatch for Special Operations Forces. The vendor currently provides innovative techniques to aggregate, analyze, and exploit vast amounts of open source data to support mission requirements. Using a combination of innovative big data technologies and experienced intelligence analysts, the vendor provides software solutions as well as training and mentoring that enable exploitation of open source information and fusion with multiple data sources.

This includes research and development activities focused on human, social, cultural, and behavioral data modeling and technology development. The vendor is providing advanced research in handling data ambiguity and varying levels of data specificity in sociocultural data sets and developing a methodology for

sociocultural data fusion and visualization. This research enables mission planners to layer information from all levels to determine the best course of action, taking information from analysis to action. Layering information from both the classified and unclassified realms allows planners to use cutting edge technology to determine named and tactical areas of interest. This capability will further facilitate analysis and exploitation during virtual operational preparation of the environment and virtual intelligence preparation of the battlefield.

IWS Fiscal Year 2013 Project Funding ($17.6M)

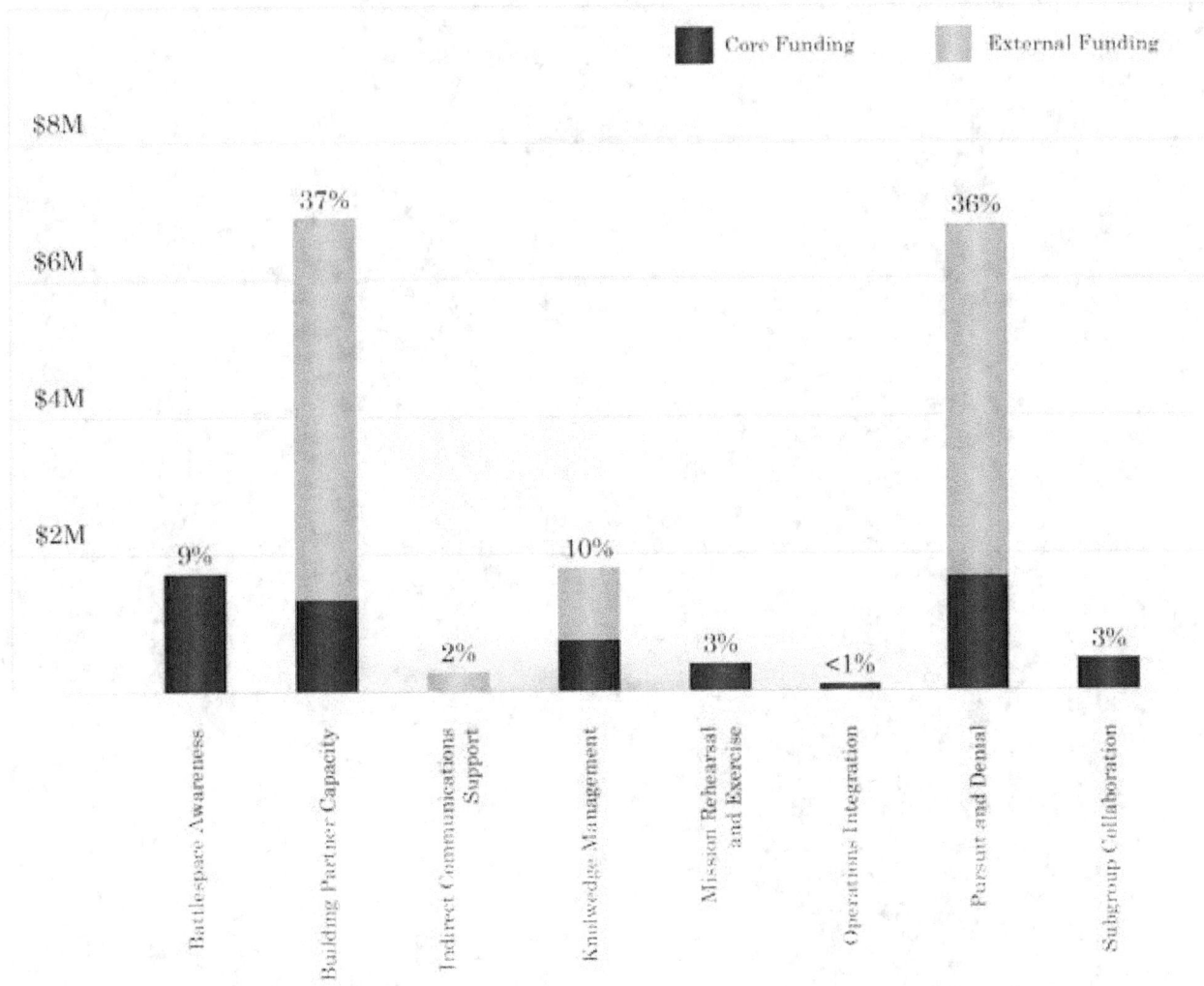

APPENDIX

CTTSO Transition and Innovation Office

Technology Transition

Technology transition is the process of taking a technology from the developmental and prototype phase to production and deployment by the end user community. Transition success is achieved when research and development products have evolved to the commercial market and/or have been inserted into government acquisition programs and can be easily and continuously obtained by the combating terrorism community. The path from the research and development phase to transition success can be challenging, and it is the mission of the Technology Transition Office at CTTSO to help overcome transition challenges to ensure success for the developers and end users. The Technology Transition Office at CTTSO works with internal program managers, external government agencies, end users, industry, and developers to overcome any barriers that may prohibit the successful transition of CTTSO technologies.

Planning for technology transition starts at the beginning of the CTTSO business cycle and continues throughout the lifecycle of the program. In order to increase the likelihood of transition success, technology transition plans are developed to provide a framework for how the technology will transition to the commercial market and/or government acquisition. Topics discussed in the Technology Transition Plan include:

- The capability gap addressed by the development of the technology;
- Identifying customers and defining the market size;
- Understanding and managing intellectual property and data rights;
- Production strategies, including partnering, investment capital, and licensing;
- Commercialization and affordability;
- Environment, safety and regulatory issues;
- Security and export control provisions;
- Test and evaluation planning and independent operational testing; and
- Operational suitability and operational support planning.

The keys to accelerating the complicated process of moving many prototypes to production includes having a disciplined process, available assistance, and teamwork among the project manager, technology transition managers, and developers. Additional information is available at the Technology Transition section of the CTTSO website: http://www.cttso.gov.

Innovation

In order to continue as a leader of delivering novel and unique technologies, CTTSO has developed a special focus on innovative ways of conducting business and delivering advanced capabilities to front-line personnel. Innovation for CTTSO customers no longer resides in the traditional national security research, development, test, and evaluation space. Novel solutions come from individual entrepreneurs and tinkerers, and in order to leverage those solutions, CTTSO must constantly look for ways to actively engage them.

In the current budget environment of focusing on doing more with less, the need for innovation increases as we look for new ways to combat terrorism. The Innovation program at CTTSO has, at its core, the following mission:

- Identify new ways to pay for success, rather than uncertain development, through prizes, challenges, and other rewards;
- Provide additional tools and resources to fulfill operational capability gaps;

- Increase the number and diversity of solution providers; and
- Provide rapid and agile ways of doing business that lower both the cost and risk of government R&D programs.

Innovation is not a destination; it is a model that enables government R&D programs to identify the best solutions in the shortest amount of time possible while being good stewards of U.S. taxpayer dollars. In 2013, CTTSO made great strides in expanding on innovative ways of conducting business. The following initiatives are underway at CTTSO to support the Innovation program:

- **CTTSO participation in the FY13 Rapid Innovation Program**: Facilitates the rapid insertion of innovative small business technologies into government systems or programs that meet critical national security needs.

- **Challenges/Prizes**: Crowdsourcing innovation problems to the world to provide ideas and solutions to fulfill important scientific and technical challenges.

- **In-Q-Tel**: Not-for-profit strategic investor who identifies, adapts, and delivers innovative commercial technology solutions to support the missions of the U.S. government.

- **Small Business Innovative Research, Phase II Enhancement**: CTTSO is engaged with multiple SBIR offices across DoD to assist in transitioning SBIR Phase II programs into marketplace.

- **2013 Global Security Challenge**: Identifies promising small business concept projects from around the world to provide next generation cyber security.

BAA Information Delivery System (BIDS)

The Broad Agency Announcement (BAA) Information Delivery System, better known as BIDS, works to support the CTTSO mission through the electronic publication of its annual BAAs. BAAs are the solicitation method of choice to bring the most urgent combating terrorism requirements forward for publication. CTTSO staff monitors BAA package instruction in light of submitter responses and feedback, and CTTSO implements improvements as needed each year to clarify the submission process.

To ensure the widest possible distribution to potential submitters, BAAs can be downloaded at the BIDS website (http://www.bids.cttso.gov) and are also advertised at the Federal Business Opportunities website (http://www.fedbizopps.gov). In addition to conventional government solicitation notices, the BIDS website provides a BIDS Advisory and Announcement area that posts BAA news, coming events, and partnering agency solicitations. In addition to the advisory, the RSS (really simple syndication) news feed allows interested users to receive real-time broadcast information at a local computer when connected to the Internet.

BIDS is a rich source of submitter information, providing small business outreach, online help, and guidance for offerers proposing the use of human subjects in research. Overall BAA statistics are posted once the BAA closes.

BIDS not only functions as a response collection system, but also provides for submission evaluation and submitter notification. Submitter data is fully protected in a 128-bit encrypted environment. Evaluators must comply with source selection data handling requirements and accept a nondisclosure agreement to access BIDS. In addition to the nondisclosure, evaluators must also certify that there is no conflict of interest before access is granted to any submissions. The evaluation process is monitored for timely notice to submitters with the typical response via an automated e-notice complete within 90 days.

BIDS continues to serve as a leading solicitation process model for other federal programs by providing a streamlined electronic solution to receive proposals, providing access for subject matter evaluation, processing submissions through the approving authority, notifying the submitter of status, and maintaining a record of solicitation results.

2013 Membership

Advanced Analytic Capabilities

Intelligence Community

- Office of the Director of National Intelligence

U.S. Department of Defense

- Defense Intelligence Agency
- Joint Chiefs of Staff
- Naval Post Graduate School, Monterey
- Naval Post Graduate School, SOCOM
- National Defense University
- Office of the Secretary of Defense (Rapid Fielding Office)
- Office of the Secretary of Defense for Special Operations/Low-Intensity Conflict

- United States Special Operations Command
- U.S. Army Training and Doctrine Command/ Intelligence Support Activity
- U.S. Marine Corps, Headquarters Marine Corps Intelligence Department
- U.S. Naval Special Warfare Group 10

U.S. Department of Homeland Security

- Customs and Border Protection
- Immigration and Customs Enforcement

U.S. Department of State

- Center for Strategic Counterterrorism Communications

Chemical, Biological, Radiological, Nuclear, and Explosives

Environmental Protection Agency

Federal Reserve Board

Intelligence Community

InterAgency Board

State and Local Agencies:

- Arlington County (VA) Fire Department
- Fairfax City (VA) Fire Department
- Fairfax County (VA) Fire and Rescue Department
- Fairfax County (VA) Police Department
- Fire Department, City of New York
- New York City Police Department
- NYC Office of Chief Medical Examiner
- Seattle (WA) Fire Department

U.S. Department of Agriculture

- Animal and Plant Health Inspection Service
- Food Safety and Inspection Service

U.S. Capitol Police

U.S. Department of Commerce

- National Institute of Standards and Technology

U.S. Department of Defense

- Assistant to the Secretary of Defense for Nuclear and Chemical and Biological Defense; Acquisition, Technology and Logistics
- Defense Advanced Research Projects Agency
- Defense Intelligence Agency
- Defense Threat Reduction Agency
- Joint Chiefs of Staff
- Joint Improvised Explosive Device Defeat Organization
- Joint Program Executive Office for Chemical and Biological Defense

- National Security Agency
- Pentagon Force Protection Agency
- Special Operations Command
- U.S. Air Force Air Combat Command
- U.S. Army ARDEC Picatinny Arsenal
- U.S. Army 20th Support Command – Chemical, Biological, Radiological, Nuclear, and high yield Explosives (CBRNE)
- U.S. Army 22nd Chemical Battalion
- U.S. Army Chemical School, Maneuver Support Center
- U.S. Army Medical Department
- U.S. Army National Ground Intelligence Center
- U.S. Army Research, Development, and Engineering Command – Edgewood Chemical Biological Center
- U.S. Marine Corps Chemical Biological Incident Response Force
- U.S. Marine Corps Explosive Ordnance Disposal
- U.S. Marine Corps Systems Command
- U.S. Navy Bureau of Medicine
- U.S. Navy Naval Air Warfare Center
- NSWC Indian Head Explosive Ordnance Disposal Technology Division
- U.S. Navy Naval Forces Central Command
- U.S. Navy Naval Research Laboratory
- U.S. Navy Naval Surface Warfare Center

U.S. Department of Energy
- National Nuclear Security Administration
- Office of Health, Safety and Security

U.S. Department of Health and Human Services
- Centers for Disease Control and Prevention
- Food and Drug Administration
- National Institute for Occupational Safety and Health

U.S. Department of Homeland Security
- Federal Emergency Management Agency
- Federal Protective Service
- Science and Technology Directorate
- Transportation Security Administration
- Transportation Security Laboratory
- U.S. Coast Guard
- U.S. Secret Service

U.S. Department of the Interior
- National Park Service, United States Park Police

U.S. Department of Labor

U.S. Department of Justice
- Bureau of Alcohol, Tobacco, Firearms and Explosives
- Federal Bureau of Investigation
- National Institute of Justice
- U.S. Marshals Service

U.S. Department of State
- Bureau of Arms Control, Verification, and Compliance
- Bureau of Diplomatic Security
- Bureau of Overseas Buildings Operations
- Counterterrorism Office

U.S. Department of Transportation
- Research and Innovative Technology Administration (Volpe Center)

U.S. Senate Sergeant at Arms

White House
- Homeland Security Council
- Office of Science and Technology Policy

Improvised Device Defeat

Intelligence Community

National Bomb Squad Commanders Advisory Board

State and Local Agencies

- Fairfax County (VA) Police Department
- Pentagon Force Protection Agency Bomb Squad (VA)
- Maryland State Police
- Michigan State Police
- Bloomington, Minnesota Police Department (Central region)
- Houston, Texas Police Department (Western region)
- Morris County Sheriff's Office (Eastern region)
- Georgia Bureau of Investigation (Southern region)

U.S. Capitol Police

U.S. Department of Defense

- U.S. Air Force Air Combat Command
- U.S. Army 52nd Ordnance Group
- U.S. Army Explosive Ordnance Disposal Technical Detachment
- U.S. Marine Corps Chemical Biological Incident Response Force
- U.S. Marine Corps Explosive Ordnance Disposal Detachment
- U.S. Navy Explosive Ordnance Disposal Detachment 63
- U.S. Navy Explosive Ordnance Disposal Fleet Liaison Office
- NSWC Indian Head Explosive Ordnance Disposal Technology Division

U.S. Department of Homeland Security

- Border and Transportation Security Directorate
- Homeland Security Advanced Research Project Agency
- Information Analysis and Infrastructure Protection Directorate
- Office for Domestic Preparedness
- Science and Technology Directorate
- U.S. Secret Service
- Transportation Security Administration
- U.S. Coast Guard

U.S. Department of Justice

- Bureau of Alcohol, Tobacco, Firearms and Explosives
- Federal Bureau of Investigation
- U.S. Marshals Service
- National Institute of Justice

Investigative and Forensic Science

Environmental Protection Agency

- National Enforcement Investigations Center

Federal Reserve Board

Intelligence Community

National Forensic Science Technology Center

National Transportation Safety Board

Senate Sergeant at Arms

U.S. Department of Commerce

- National Institute of Standards and Technology – Office of Law Enforcement Standards

U.S. Department of Defense

- Component Commands
- Defense Advanced Research Projects Agency
- Defense Computer Forensics Laboratory
- Defense Cyber Crime Institute
- Defense Forensics and Biometrics Agency
- Defense Forensic Science Center
- Defense Forensic Enterprise (OUSD(ATL))
- Defense Intelligence Agency
- Defense Threat Reduction Agency
- Headquarters, U.S. Marine Corps
- Joint IED Defeat Organization
- Intelligence Systems Support Office (OUSD(I) ECTI)
- National Center for Credibility Assessment
- National Geospatial Intelligence Agency
- National Media Exploitation Center
- Naval Research Laboratory
- Office of the Provost Marshal General
- Pentagon Force Protection Agency
- U.S. Air Force Office of Special Investigations
- U.S. Army Criminal Investigation Command
- U.S. Navy Naval Criminal Investigative Service
- U.S. Special Operations Command

U.S. Department of Energy

- Office of Health, Safety, and Security

U.S. Department of Health and Human Services

- Office of Inspector General

U.S. Department of Homeland Security

- Customs and Border Protection
- Federal Emergency Management Agency
- Federal Protective Service
- Immigration and Customs Enforcement (including Homeland Security Investigations Forensic Laboratory)
- U.S. Secret Service
- Transportation Security Administration (including Transportation Security Laboratory)

U.S. Department of Justice

- Bureau of Alcohol, Tobacco, Firearms, and Explosives
- Drug Enforcement Administration
- Federal Bureau of Investigation
- National Institute of Justice
- U.S. Marshals Service

U.S. Department of State

- Office of the Coordinator for Counterterrorism

U.S. Department of Transportation

- Federal Aviation Administration

U.S. Postal Inspection Service

U.S. Department of Veterans Affairs

Personnel Protection

Intelligence Community

Federal Bureau of Investigation

U.S. Capitol Police

U.S. Department of Commerce

- National Institute of Standards and Technology
- Office of Law Enforcement Standards

U.S. Department of Defense

- Defense Threat Reduction Agency
- Joint Improvised Explosive Device Defeat Organization
- Joint Personnel Recovery Agency
- Pentagon Force Protection Agency
- Rapid Reaction Technology Office
- U.S. Air Force Office of Special Investigations
- U.S. Army
- U.S. Army Criminal Investigation Command
- U.S. Army Joint Trauma Analysis and Prevention of Injury in Combat
- U.S. Army Medical Research and Material Command
- U.S. Army Program Executive Office Soldier Protective Equipment
- U.S. Army Research, Development and Engineering Command
- U.S. Army Research Laboratory
- U.S. Army Soldier Systems Center (Natick)
- U.S. Army Special Operations Command

- U.S. Army Tank Automotive Research, Development and Engineering Center
- U.S. Navy Naval Air Systems Command
- U.S. Navy Naval Criminal Investigative Service
- U.S. Navy Program Executive Office Ships

U.S. Department of Energy

U.S. Department of Homeland Security

- Customs and Border Protection
- Federal Air Marshal Service
- Federal Law Enforcement Training Center
- U.S. Secret Service, Special Services Division, Technical Security Division

U.S. Department of Justice

- Marshals Service
- National Institute of Justice

U.S. Department of State

Physical Security

Environmental Protection Agency

Federal Reserve Board

Intelligence Community

State and Local Agencies

- DC Metropolitan Police
- Jacksonville (FL) Port Authority
- Lynchburg (VA) Sheriff's Office
- New York Police Department
- Pinellas County (FL) Sheriff's Office
- Port Authority of New York & New Jersey
- Protective Services Police Department
- U.S. Capitol Police

U.S. Department of Agriculture

- Forest Service

U.S. Department of Commerce

- National Institute of Standards and Technology

U.S. Department of Defense

- Defense Advanced Research Projects Agency
- Defense Intelligence Agency
- Defense Threat Reduction Agency
- Explosives Safety Board
- Joint Chiefs of Staff

- Joint Improvised Explosive Device Defeat Organization
- Joint Task Force North (NORTHCOM)
- Joint Warfare Analysis Center (JWAC)
- National Reconnaissance Office
- Offices of the Secretary of Defense
- Physical Security Equipment Action Group
- Unified Combatant Commands
- U.S. Air Force Research Laboratory
- U.S. Army Armaments Research, Development and Engineering Center
- U.S. Army Asymmetric Warfare Group
- U.S. Army Chemical School
- U.S. Army Corps of Engineers
- U.S. Army Maneuver and Support Center
- U.S. Army Office of the Provost Marshal General
- U.S. Army Product Manager-Force Protection Systems
- U.S. Army Product Manager-Guardian
- U.S. Army Rapid Equipping Force
- U.S. Army Research, Development and Engineering Command
- U.S. Army Research Laboratory
- U.S. Army Special Forces Command
- U.S. Army Special Operations Command
- U.S. Army Training and Doctrine Command
- U.S. Marine Corps Central Command
- U.S. Marine Corps Special Operations Command
- U.S. Marine Corps Systems Command
- U.S. Marine Corps Warfighting Laboratory
- U.S. Navy Chief of Naval Operations
- U.S. Navy Commander Navy Installations Command
- U.S. Navy Criminal Investigative Service
- U.S. Navy Expeditionary Combat Command

- U.S. Navy Explosive Ordnance Disposal Technology Division
- U.S. Naval Facilities Engineering Command
- U.S. Naval Facilities Engineering Service Center
- U.S. Navy Office of Naval Research
- U.S. Navy Sea Systems Command
- U.S. Navy Strategic Systems Programs
- U.S. Navy Surface Warfare Center

U.S. Department of Energy

- Lawrence Livermore National Laboratory
- National Nuclear Security Administration
- Nuclear Regulatory Commission

U.S. Department of Homeland Security

- Coast Guard
- Customs and Border Protection
- Immigration and Customs Enforcement
- Science and Technology Directorate
- Secret Service
- Transportation Security Administration
- Transportation Security Laboratory

U.S. Department of the Interior

- Bureau of Reclamation

U.S. Department of Justice

- Bureau of Alcohol, Tobacco, Firearms and Explosives
- Drug Enforcement Administration
- Federal Bureau of Investigation
- Federal Bureau of Prisons

U.S. Department of State

- Bureau of Diplomatic Security

U.S. Department of Transportation

Surveillance, Collection, and Operations Support

Intelligence Community

U.S. SOCOM

Tactical Operations Support

Intelligence Community

National Tactical Officers Association

State and Local Law Enforcement

- Boston SWAT
- Maryland State Police SWAT
- Massachusetts State Police
- NYPD
- FDNY
- South Carolina State Police SWAT

U.S. Department of Defense

- Defense Intelligence Agency
- Joint IED Defeat Organization
- Joint Personnel Recovery Agency
- National Guard Bureau
- U.S. Air Force
- U.S. Army
    - ARDEC Picatinny Arsenal
    - Asymmetric Warfare Group
    - 20th Support Command (CBRNE)
    - Night Vision Labs
    - PEO Soldier
    - Rapid Equipping Force
    - Soldier Systems Center
- U.S. Marine Corps
    - Marine Corps Forces Cyber Command

- U.S. Navy
- U.S. Special Operations Command
    - Theater Special Operations Commands

U.S. Department of Energy

- National Nuclear Security Administration

U.S. Department of Homeland Security

- Federal Air Marshals Service
- Office of Bombing Prevention
- U.S. Bureau of Customs and Border Protection
    - Border Patrol Tactical Unit
- U.S. Coast Guard
- U.S. Secret Service
- U.S. Immigration and Customs Enforcement/ Homeland Security Investigations

U.S. Department of Justice

- Federal Bureau of Investigation
    - Hostage Rescue Team
    - Ballistic Research Facility
- U.S. Marshals Service
- Bureau of Alcohol, Tobacco, Firearms and Explosives
    - Special Response Team

U.S. Department of State

Training Technology Development

Intelligence Community

InterAgency Board

National Bomb Squad Commanders Advisory Board

National Tactical Officers Association

United States Agency for International Development

U.S. Department of Defense

- Joint Improvised Explosive Device Defeat Office
- Office of the Undersecretary of Defense for Personnel and Readiness
- Pentagon Force Protection Agency
- Defense Intelligence Agency
- U.S. Army Asymmetric Warfare Group
- U.S. Army John F. Kennedy Special Warfare Center and School
- U.S. Army Special Operations Command
- U.S. Marine Corps
- U.S. Marine Training and Education Command

- U.S. Naval Special Warfare Command
- U.S. Special Operations Command

U.S. Department of Homeland Security

- Customs and Border Protection
- Homeland Security Investigations
- Office for Bombing Prevention
- Science and Technology Directorate
- Secret Service
- Transportation Security Administration
- Federal Law Enforcement Training Center

U.S. Department of Justice

- Bureau of Alcohol, Tobacco, Firearms, and Explosives
- Federal Bureau of Investigation
- U.S. Marshals Service

U.S. Department of State

- Bureau of Diplomatic Security

Explosive Ordnance Disposal/Low-Intensity Conflict

- Joint Service Explosive Ordnance Disposal
- Naval Sea Systems Command
- Navy Expeditionary Combat Command
- U.S. Special Operations Command

2013 Performers

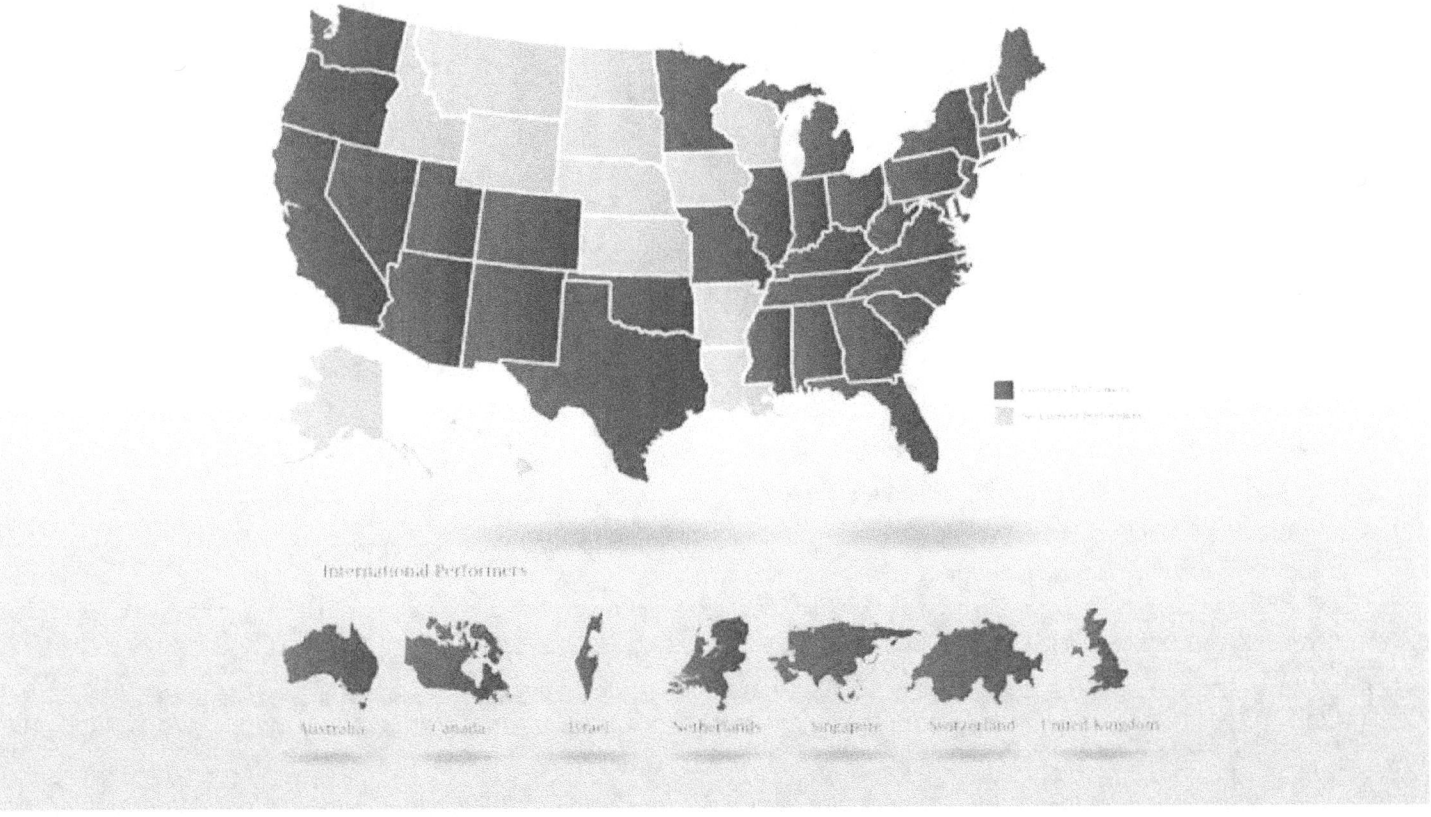

International Performers

Australia   Canada   Israel   Netherlands   Singapore   Switzerland   United Kingdom

Alabama

Army Space and Missile Defense Command, Huntsville

Redstone Arsenal, Redstone Arsenal

Arizona

Nivisys Industries, LLC, Tempe

California

Aerovironment, Inc., Simi Valley

Altobridge Corporation, San Jose

Decision Sciences International Corporation, Poway

General Dynamics Ordnance and Tactical Systems, Healdsburg

Naval Facilities Engineering Service Center, Port Hueneme

Naval Air Warfare Center, China Lake

Naval Post Graduate School, Monterey

Palantir USG, Inc., Palo Alto

Precision Optics Corporation, Torrance

Quantum Magnetics Inc., San Diego

Rapiscan Systems Laboratories, Inc., Sunnyvale

Science Applications International Corporation, San Diego

Smiths Detection, Pasadena

Spectral Labs, Inc., San Diego

System Technology, Inc., Hawthorne

Toyon Research Corporation, Goleta

Colorado

Applied Research Associates, Inc., Littleton

APTEK, Colorado Springs

NEK Advanced Securities Group, Inc., Colorado Springs

Rocky Mountain Scientific Laboratories, Littleton

Stratom, Inc., Boulder

Connecticut

Ensign-Bickford Aerospace & Defense Co., Simsbury

District of Columbia

Bureau of Alcohol, Tobacco, Firearms and Explosives

Naval Research Laboratory, Washington D.C.

Florida

Air Force Research Laboratory, Tyndall Air Force Base

AMP Research, Inc., Naples

CTC Tampa Bay, Largo

Cubic Defense Applications, Orlando

Florida International University, Miami

Florida State University, Panama City

Forensic Innovation Center, Largo

National Forensic Science Technology Center, Largo

Naval Surface Warfare Center, Panama City

Navy Experimental Dive Unit, Panama City

Ocean Optics Spectroscopy, Dunedin, FL

Sealund & Associates Corporation, St. Petersburg

Studio 14B, LLC, Safety Harbor, FL

Unconventional Concepts, Inc., Mary Esther, FL

Georgia

Georgia Tech Research Institute, Atlanta

Squires-Fulcher LLC, Locust Grove

Illinois

Argonne National Laboratory, Argonne

University of Illinois, Urbana-Champaign

Indiana

Naval Surface Warfare Center, Crane

Kentucky

Oakridge National Laboratory,

Maine

Falcon Performance Footwear, Auburn

Monroe Infrared Technology, Inc., Kennebunk

Maryland

Army CERDEC, I2WD, Aberdeen MD

Army Research Laboratory, Aberdeen Proving Ground

Avon Protection Systems, Inc., Aberdeen

Edgewood Chemical Biological Center, Aberdeen Proving Ground

Garrison, Adelphi Laboratory Center IMNE-ALC-RMO, Hagerstown

Hardwire LLC, Pocomoke City

Mistral Security Incorporated, Bethesda

Naval Air Warfare Command, Patuxent River

Naval Air Warfare Center, Patuxent River

Naval Explosive Ordnance Disposal Technology Division, Indian Head

Naval Surface Warfare Center, Indian Head

Oceaneering International Inc., Hanover

Roboteam North America

U.S. Army Aberdeen Test Center

W.L. Gore, Elkton

Massachusetts

Aptima, Woburn

Artisent, Inc., Boston

BAE Systems, Burlington

C-2i, Inc., Stow

Charles River Analytics Inc., Cambridge

ENSR International Corporation, Westford

Excellims Corporation, Maynard

Flir Government Systems, Boston

Morpho Detection, Wilmington

Physical Sciences Inc, Andover

QinetiQ – North America, Inc., Waltham

Thermo Fisher Scientific, Inc., Wilmington

Whitehead Institute for Biomedical Research, Cambridge

Michigan

Avon Protection Systems, Inc., Cadillac

Baker Enterprises, Alpena

Cybernet Systems Corporation, Ann Arbor

Quantum Signal LLC, Ann Arbor

Quantum Signal, Saline

Minnesota

University of Minnesota, Minneapolis

Mississippi

Stark Aerospace, Starkville

U.S. Army Engineer Research and Development Center, Vicksburg

Missouri

Midwest Research Institute, Kansas City

Washington University in St. Louis, St. Louis

Nevada

Remote Sensing Laboratory, Las Vegas

Sierra Pacific Innovations, Las Vegas

New Hampshire

Elbit Systems of America – Kollsman, Merrimack

Globe Manufacturing Company, Pittsfield

HALO Maritime Defense Systems, Newton

Sig Sauer, Inc., Exeter

New Jersey

Armament Research, Development and Engineering Center, Picatinny Arsenal

Goodrich Corporation Sensors Unlimited, Inc., Princeton

Structured Materials Industries, Piscataway

New Mexico

Applied Research Associates, Inc., Albuquerque

Energetic Materials Research and Testing Center, Socorro

National Assessment Group, Kirtland Air Force Base

Sandia National Laboratories, Albuquerque

White Sands Missile Range

New York

GE Global Research, Niskayuna

Kitware, Inc., Clifton Park

Persistent Systems, LLC, New York

North Carolina

Advanced Mission Systems, Charlotte

Atlantic Aero, Greensboro

Bilingual Communications, Inc., Cary

North Carolina State University, Textile Protection and Comfort Center, Raleigh

Ohio

AlphaMicron, Kent

Battelle Memorial Institute, Columbus

Lion Apparel, Dayton

Oklahoma

Southwest Research Institute, Midwest City

Oregon

P&R Technologies, Inc., Portland

Pennsylvania

DRS Laurel Technologies, Johnstown

Getting More, Inc., Philadelphia

RE2 Inc., Pittsburgh

University of Pennsylvania

Rhode Island

Naval Undersea Warfare Center, Newport

South Carolina

Advanced Mission Systems, Fort Mill

Asymmetric Combat Institute, Taylors

Tennessee

Universal Strategy Group, Inc., Mt. Pleasant

Texas

Accuracy 1st, Inc., Arthur City

Applied Research Associates, Inc., San Antonio

DetectaChem, Houston

G2 Associates, Heath

Infrared Cameras, Inc., Beaumont

International Personnel Protection, Inc., Austin

K2Share, LLC, College Station

Laser Shot, Inc., Stafford

Praevius Group, Salado

Protection Engineering Consultants, LLC, Austin

Southwest Research Institute, San Antonio

Texas A&M University, College Station

Utah

Coda Octopus USA, Salt Lake City

Torion Technologies, Inc., American Fork

Vermont

Sound Innovations, Inc., White River Junction

Virginia

Adayana Government Group, Falls Church

Adgraphics, Alexandria, VA

Battelle Memorial Institute, Arlington

Blackbird Technologies, Herndon

Black Tree, Ashburn

The Bode Technology Group, Inc, Lorton

Conflict Kinetics, Reston

Dager Technology, Arlington

Defense Threat Reduction Agency, Ft. Belvoir

Federal Bureau of Investigation, Quantico

Gatekeeper, Inc., Sterling

Intelligent Decision Partners, LLC, Reston

Joint Non-Lethal Weapons Directorate, Quantico

ManTech International Corporation, Chantilly

Master Print, Inc., Newington

McQ, Inc., Fredericksburg

Naval Surface Warfare Center, Dahlgren

National Crash Analysis Center of George Washington University, Ashburn

Night Vision and Electronic Sensors Directorate, Ft. Belvoir

Northrop Grumman Training Solutions Sector, Herndon

S4 Tech, Reston

Science Applications International Corporation, McLean

Segue Technologies, Arlington

System of Systems Analytics, Inc., Fairfax

Trident Systems, Inc., Fairfax, VA

White Canvas Group, Arlington

White Canvas Group, Alexandria

Washington

The Boeing Company, Seattle

Cascade Designs, Inc., Seattle

Pacific Northwest Laboratory, Richland

Sound Metrics Corporation, Lake Forest Park

Stark Aerospace, Redmond

West Virginia

Azimuth Inc., Morgantown

STS International, Berkeley Springs

West Virginia National Guard, Camp Dawson

International

Australia

Australian Government Department of the Prime Minister and Cabinet

Catapult Innovations, Scoresby, Victoria

ChemCentre, Bentley, Western Australia

Defense Science and Technology Organization, Canberra

Defence Science and Technology Organisation, Edinburgh

Defense Science and Technology Organization – Fisherman's Bend, Melbourne, Victoria

Department of Prime Minister Cabinet, Canberra

Emergency Management Australia, Canberra

Flinders University, Adelaide

Queensland Fire and Rescue Services, Brisbane, Queensland

Queensland University of Technology, Brisbane, Queensland

Semantic Science Pty Ltd, Stirling

University of Adelaide, Adelaide, South Australia

University of Canberra, Canberra

University of Tasmania, Hobart, Tasmania

University of Technology, Sydney, New South Wales

Canada

AirBoss-Defence, Acton Vale, Quebec

Biokinetics & Associates Ltd, Ontario

Canadian Border Services Agency, Ottawa, Ontario

Defence Research and Development Canada, Suffield

Defence Research and Development Canada, Valcartier, Quebec

Oculus, Toronto, ON

Public Health Agency Canada, Winnipeg, Manitoba

Royal Canadian Mounted Police, Ottawa, Ontario

Toronto Police

Transport Canada, Ottawa, Ontario

Israel

Assatec Inc.

DEA Research and Development, Ltd, Jerusalem

Elbit Land/Platforms, Yokne'am

Electro-Optics Industries, Ltd., Rehovot

The Hebrew University of Jersusalem, Jerusalem

Israel Defense Force

Israel Ministry of Defense, Tel Aviv

Israeli National Police, Jerusalem

Israeli Security Agency, Tel Aviv

National Information Security Authority

National Nuclear Research Center, Negev

National Israeli Security Agency, Tel Aviv

PrevenTech, Ltd, Jerusalem

Roboteam, Tel-Aviv

Soltam Systems, Ltd., Yokne'am

Tamar Explosives

Netherlands

Nederlandse Organisatie voor Toegepast Natuurwetenschappelijk Onderzoek (TNO) (Netherlands Organisation for Applied Scientific Research)

Singapore

Defence Science and Technology Agency

Switzerland

Artkis Radiation Detectors Ltd, Zurich

United Kingdom

Buckler Davies Consultancy Limited, Swindon

Centre for the Protection of National Infrastructure

Cobalt Light Systems

Defence Science and Technology Laboratory, Fort Halstead, Kent

Defence Science and Technology Laboratories, Porton Down

Hazard Management Solutions, Inc., Farington, Oxfordshire

Home Office Scientific Development Branch, London

LGC Limited, Middlesex

MBDA, Bristol

Ministry of Defence Counter Terrorism Science and Technology Centre, Salisbury

Serious Organized Crime Agency, London

ThruVision/Digital Barriers, London

UK Ministry of Defence

Glossary of Acronyms

AAC	Advanced Analytic Capabilities
ACG-PD	Assistant Commanding General for Police Development
AITSS	Advanced Inline Thermal Sniper Sight
AOR	Area of Operation
ARA	Applied Research Associates
ASD SO/LIC	Assistant Secretary of Defense for Special Operations/Low-Intensity Conflict
AWC	Automatic Wire Cutter
BABT	Behind Armor Blunt Trauma
BFS	Backface Signature
BFT	Blue Force Tracking
BRITE	Biometrics, Recognition, Identity Management, Tracking, and Exploitation
CADENA	Cross-Agency Distributed Edge Network Analytic Platform
CAMMI	Culturally Authentic Materials Management between Institutions
CAPEX	Capability Exercise
CB	Chemical and Biological
CBR	Chemical, Biological, and Radiological
CBRN	Chemical, Biological, Radiological, and Nuclear
CBRNE	Chemical, Biological, Radiological, Nuclear, and Explosives
C-IED	Counter Improvised Explosive Device
CNT	Carbon Nanotube
CNVD-SF	Clip-On Night Vision Device – Sensor Fusion
CTTSO	Combating Terrorism Technical Support Office
DARPA	Defense Advanced Research Projects Agency

DHS S&T	Department of Homeland Security Science and Technology Directorate
DoD	Department of Defense
DOS	Department of State
EOD	Explosive Ordnance Disposal
EOD/LIC	Explosive Ordnance Disposal/Low-Intensity Conflict
EMTAS	Enhanced Mortar Targeting System
EPME	Evidence-Based Planning, Monitoring, and Evaluation
FD	FirstDefender
FEBR	Forced Entry Ballistic Blast Resistant
FY	Fiscal Year
GC-MS	Gas Chromatography-Mass Spectrometer
GCS	Ground Control Station
GF	Green Field
HAHO	High Altitude – High Opening
HALO	High Altitude – Low Opening
HBPR&A	Human Behavior Pattern Recognition and Analysis
He-3	Helium-3
HISTARS	Handheld Intelligence Surveillance Target Acquisition Reconnaissance System
HME	Homemade Explosives
HRP	High-Risk Personnel
ICE	Integrated Conveyance Escort
ICT	Information and Communication Technology
IED	Improvised Explosive Device
IDD	Improved Diver Display
IDD	Improvised Device Defeat

IFS	Investigative and Forensic Science
IG/T	Interdepartmental Group on Terrorism
IHE	Insensitive High Explosive
iLive	inLine Instant Video Enhancement
INS	Instant Notification System
IO	Information Operations
IPP	International Personnel Protection
IR	Infrared
ISR	Intelligence, Surveillance, and Reconnaissance
IT-SAT	Insider Threat Situational Awareness Training
IWG/CT	Interagency Working Group on Counterterrorism
IWS	Irregular Warfare Support
LOOM	Linking Outputs to Outcome Model
MADFKP	Modular Air Droppable Force Protection Kit
MANET	Mobile Ad Hoc Network
MDP	Ministerial Development Plans
MFE	Multi-Functional Earpiece
MISO	Military Information Support Operations
MPAE	Metrics Progress Analysis Engine
MPC	Media Production Center
MS&G	Models, Simulations, and Games
MTGR	Micro Tactical Ground Robot
NBSCAB	National Bomb Squad Commanders Advisory Board
NFPA	National Fire Protection Association
NG-TacMN	Next Generation Tactical Mesh Network

NIR	Near Infrared
NTM-A	NATO Training Mission – Afghanistan
OTD	Orthogonal TIC Detector
PAPR	Powered Air Purifying Respirator
PBIED	Person-Borne Improvised Explosive Device
PMES	Political, Military, Economic, Social
PMESII	Political, Military, Economic, Social, Infrastructure, and Information
PP	Personnel Protection
PS	Physical Security
R&D	Research and Development
RDD	Radiological Dispersion Device
ROCU	Ruggedized Operator Control Unit
S-CAPS	Sociocultural Awareness through Passive Sensing
SCBA	Self-Contained Breathing Apparatus
SCOS	Surveillance, Collection, and Operations Support
SF	Special Forces
SIDD	Scalable Improvised Device Defeat
SNAP	Social Network Analysis Platform
SNR	Signal to Noise
SOCOM	Special Operations Command
SOF	Special Operations Forces
SSE	Sensitive Site Exploitation
SUNet	Secure Unclassified Network
SWBCIEDWG	Southwest Border C-IED Working Group
SWIR	Short Wave Infrared

TCO	Transnational Criminal Organizations
TIC	Toxic Industrial Chemicals
TOS	Tactical Operations Support
TRG	Technical Response Group
TSWG	Technical Support Working Group
TTD	Training Technology Development
UAS	Unmanned Aerial System
UBA	Underwater Breathing Apparatus
VBIED	Vehicle-Borne Improvised Explosive Device
WASP	West African Sharing Portal